The Birth of Tragedy out of the Spirit of Music: An Attempt at Self-Criticism

Start Publishing PD LLC
Copyright © 2024 by Start Publishing PD LLC

All rights reserved, including the right to reproduce this book or portions thereof in any form whatsoever.

Start Publishing PD is a registered trademark of Start Publishing PD LLC
Manufactured in the United States of America

Cover art: Shutterstock/Taisiya Kozorez

Cover design: Jennifer Do

10 9 8 7 6 5 4 3 2 1

ISBN 979-8-8809-1337-4

The Birth of Tragedy out of the Spirit of Music: An Attempt at Self-Criticism

by Friedrich Nietzsche

Translated by Ian C. Johnston

Preface to Richard Wagner

In order to keep far away from me all possible disturbances, agitation, and misunderstandings which the assembly of ideas in this piece of writing will bring about on account of the peculiar character of our aesthetic public, and also to be capable of writing a word of introduction to the book with the same contemplative joy which marks every page, the crystallization of good inspirational hours, I am imagining the look with which you, my esteemed friend, will receive this work—how you, perhaps after an evening stroll in the winter snow, look at the unbound Prometheus on the title page, read my name, and are immediately convinced that, no matter what this text consists of, the writer has something serious and urgent to say, and that, in addition, in everything which he composed, he was conversing with you as with someone present and could only write down what was appropriate to such a presence.

In this connection, you will remember that I gathered these ideas together at the same time that your marvelous commemorative volume on Beethoven appeared, that is, during the shock and grandeur of the war which had just broken out. Nevertheless, people might think that this collection of ideas has an aesthetic voluptuousness opposed to patriotic excitement, a cheerful game different from brave seriousness. Such people would be quite wrong. By actually reading the work, they should rather be astonished to recognize clearly the serious German problem which we have to deal with, the problem which we really placed right in the middle of German hopes as its vortex and turning point.

However, it will perhaps be generally offensive for these same people to see an aesthetic problem taken so seriously, if they are in a position to see art as nothing more than a merry diversion, as an easily dispensable bell-ringing summoning us to the "Seriousness of Existence," as if no one knew what such an opposing stance as this has to do with such "Seriousness of Existence."

For these serious readers, let this serve as a caution: I am convinced that art is the highest task and the essential metaphysical capability of this life, in the sense of that man to whom I here, as to my inspiring pioneer on this path, have dedicated this book.

Basel, December 1871

1

We will have achieved much for the study of aesthetics when we come, not merely to a logical understanding, but also to the immediately certain apprehension of the fact that the further development of art is bound up with the duality of the Apollonian and the Dionysian, just as reproduction depends upon the duality of the sexes, their continuing strife and only periodically occurring reconciliation. We take these names from the Greeks who gave a clear voice to the profound secret teachings of their contemplative art, not in ideas, but in the powerfully clear forms of their divine world.

With those two gods of art, Apollo and Dionysus, we link our recognition that in the Greek world there exists a huge contrast, in origins and purposes, between visual (plastic) arts, the Apollonian, and the non-visual art of music, the Dionysian. Both very different drives go hand in hand, for the most part in open conflict with each other and simultaneously provoking each other all the time to new and more powerful offspring, in order to perpetuate for themselves the contest of opposites which the common word "Art" only seems to bridge, until they finally, through a marvelous metaphysical act, seem to pair up with each other and, as this pair, produce Attic tragedy, just as much a Dionysian as an Apollonian work of art.

In order to get closer to these two instinctual drives, let us think of them next as the separate artistic worlds of dreams and of intoxication, physiological phenomena between which we can observe an opposition corresponding to the one between the Apollonian and the Dionysian.

According to the ideas of Lucretius, the marvelous divine shapes first appeared to the mind of man in a dream. It was in a dream that the great artist saw the delightful anatomy of superhuman existence, and the Hellenic poet, questioned about the secrets of poetic creativity, would have recalled his dreams and given an explanation exactly similar to the one Hans Sachs provides in Die Meistersinger.

My friend, that is precisely the poet's work— To figure out his dreams, mark them down. Believe me, the truest illusion of mankind Is revealed to him in dreams: All poetic art and poeticizing Is nothing but interpreting true dreams.

The beautiful appearance of the world of dreams, in whose creation each man is a complete artist, is the condition of all plastic art, indeed, as we shall see, an important half of poetry. We enjoy the form with an immediate understanding, all shapes speak to us, nothing is indifferent and unnecessary.

For all the very intense life of these dream realities, we nevertheless have the thoroughly disagreeable sense of their illusory quality. At least that is my experience. For their frequency, even normality, I can point to many witnesses and the utterances of poets. Even the philosophical man has the presentiment that this reality in which we live and have our being is an illusion, that under it lies hidden a second quite different reality. And Schopenhauer specifically designates as the trademark of philosophical talent the ability to recognize at certain times that human beings and all things are mere phantoms or dream pictures.

Now, just as the philosopher behaves in relation to the reality of existence, so the artistically excitable man behaves in relation to the reality of dreams. He looks at them precisely and with pleasure, for from these pictures he fashions his interpretation of life; from these events he rehearses his life. This is not merely a case of agreeable and friendly images which he experiences with a complete understanding. They also include what is serious, cloudy, sad, dark, sudden scruples, teasing accidents, nervous expectations, in short, the entire "divine comedy" of life, including the Inferno—all this moves past him, not just like a shadow play, for he lives and suffers in the midst of these scenes, yet not without that fleeting sensation of illusion. And perhaps several people remember, like me, amid the dangers and terrors of a dream, successfully cheering themselves up by shouting: "It is a dream! I want to dream it some more!" I have also heard accounts of some people who had the ability to set out the causal connection of one and the same dream over three or more consecutive nights. These facts are clear evidence showing that our innermost beings, the secret underground in all of us, experiences its dreams with deep enjoyment, as a delightful necessity.

The Greeks expressed this joyful necessity of the dream experience in their god Apollo, who, as god of all the plastic arts, is at the same time the god of prophecy. In accordance with the root meaning of his association with brightness, he is the god of light. He also rules over the beautiful appearance of the inner fantasy world. The higher truth, the perfection of this condition in contrast to the sketchy understanding of our daily reality, as well as the deep consciousness of a healing and helping nature in sleep and dreaming, is the symbolic analogy to the capacity to prophesy the truth, as well as to art in general, through which life is made possible and worth living. But also that delicate line which the dream image may not cross so as to work its effect pathologically (otherwise the illusion would deceive us as crude reality)—that line must not be absent from the image of Apollo, that boundary of moderation, that freedom from more ecstatic excitement, that fully calm wisdom of the god of images. His eye must be sun-like, in keeping with his origin. Even when he is angry and gazes with displeasure, the consecration of the beautiful illusion rests on him.

And so one may verify (in an eccentric way) what Schopenhauer says of the man trapped in the veil of Maja: "As on the stormy sea which extends without limit on all sides, howling mountainous waves rise up and sink and a sailor sits in a row boat, trusting the weak craft, so, in the midst of a world of torments, the solitary man sits peacefully, supported by and trusting in the principium individuationis [the principle of individuality]" (World as Will and Idea, Vol. I, p. 416). Yes, we could say of Apollo that the imperturbable trust in that principle and the calm sitting still of the man conscious of it attained its loftiest expression in him, and we may even designate Apollo himself as the marvelous divine image of the principium individuationis, from whose gestures and gaze all the joy and wisdom of illusion, together with its beauty, speak to us.

In the same place Schopenhauer also described for us the monstrous horror which seizes a man when he suddenly doubts his ways of comprehending illusion, when the sense of a foundation, in any one of its forms, appears to suffer a breakdown. If we add to this horror the ecstatic rapture, which rises up out of the same collapse of the principium individuationis from the innermost depths of human beings, yes, from the innermost depths of nature, then we have a glimpse into the essence of the Dionysian, which is presented to us most closely through the analogy to intoxication.

Either through the influence of narcotic drink, of which all primitive men and peoples speak, or through the powerful coming on of spring, which drives joyfully through all of nature, that Dionysian excitement arises. As its power increases, the subjective fades into complete forgetfulness of self. In the German Middle Ages under the same power of Dionysus constantly growing hordes waltzed from place to place, singing and dancing. In that St. John's and St. Vitus's dancing we recognize the Bacchic chorus of the Greeks once again, and its precursors in Asia Minor, right back to Babylon and the orgiastic Sacaea [a riotous Babylonian festival].

There are men who, from a lack of experience or out of apathy, turn mockingly away from such phenomena as from a "sickness of the people," with a sense of their own health and filled with pity. These poor people naturally do not have any sense of how deathly and ghost-like this very "Health" of theirs sounds, when the glowing life of the Dionysian throng roars past them. Under the magic of the Dionysian, not only does the bond between man and man lock itself in place once more, but also nature itself, now matter how alienated, hostile, or subjugated, rejoices again in her festival of reconciliation with her prodigal son, man. The earth freely offers up her gifts, and the beasts of prey from the rocks and the desert approach in peace. The wagon of Dionysus is covered with flowers and wreaths. Under his yolk stride panthers and tigers.

If someone were to transform Beethoven's Ode to Joy into a painting and not restrain his imagination when millions of people sink dramatically into the dust, then we could come close to the Dionysian. Now is the slave a free man, now all the stiff, hostile barriers break apart, those things which necessity and arbitrary power or "saucy fashion" have established between men. Now, with the gospel of world harmony, every man feels himself not only united with his neighbour, reconciled and fused together, but also as if the veil of Maja has been ripped apart, with only scraps fluttering around before the mysterious original unity. Singing and dancing, man expresses himself as a member of a higher unity. He has forgotten how to walk and talk and is on the verge of flying up into the air as he dances. The enchantment speaks out in his gestures. Just as the animals speak and the earth gives milk and honey, so now something supernatural echoes out of him. He feels himself a god. He now moves in a lofty ecstasy, as he saw the gods move in his dream. The man is no longer an artist. He has become a work of art. The artistic power of all of nature, the rhapsodic satisfaction of the primordial unity, reveals itself here in the intoxicated performance. The finest clay, the most expensive marble—man—is here worked and chiseled, and the cry of the Eleusianian mysteries rings out to the chisel blows of the Dionysian world artist: "Do you fall down, you millions? World, do you have a sense of your creator?"

2

Up to this point, we have considered the Apollonian and its opposite, the Dionysian, as artistic forces which break forth out of nature itself, without the mediation of the human artist and in which the human artistic drive is for the time being satisfied directly—on the one hand as a world of dream images, whose perfection has no connection with an individual's high level of intellect or artistic education, on the other hand, as the intoxicating reality, which once again does not respect the individual, but even seeks to abolish the individual and to restore him through a mystic feeling of collective unity. In comparison to these unmediated artistic states of nature, every artist is an "Imitator," and, in fact, an artist either of Apollonian dream or Dionysian intoxication or, finally, as in Greek tragedy, for example, simultaneously an artist of intoxication and dreams. As the last, it is possible for us to imagine how he sinks down in the Dionysian drunkenness and mystical obliteration of the self, alone and apart from the rapturous throng, and how through the Apollonian effects of dream his own state now reveals itself to him, that is, his unity with the innermost basis of the world, in a metaphorical dream picture.

In accordance with these general assumptions and comparisons, let us now approach the Greeks, in order to recognize to what degree and to what heights the natural artistic drives had developed in them and how we are in a position to understand more deeply and assess the relationship of the Greek artist to his primordial images or, to use Aristotle's expression, his "imitation of nature."

In spite of all their literature on dreams and numerous dream anecdotes, we can speak of the dreams of the Greeks only hypothetically, although with fair certainty. Given the incredibly clear and accurate plastic capability of their eyes, along with their intelligent and open love of colour, one cannot go wrong in assuming that (to the shame all those born later) their dreams also had a logical causality of lines and circumferences, colours, and groupings, a sequence of scenes rather like their best bas reliefs, whose perfection would justify us, if such a comparison were possible, to describe the dreaming Greek man as a Homer and Homer as a dreaming Greek man, in a deeper sense than when modern man, with respect to his dreams, has the temerity to compare himself with Shakespeare

On the other hand, we do not need to speak merely hypothetically when we have to expose the immense gap which separates the Dionysian Greeks from the Dionysian barbarians. In all quarters of the old world (setting aside here the newer worlds), from Rome to Babylon, we can confirm the existence of Dionysian celebrations, of a type, at best, related to the Greeks in much the same way as the bearded satyr whose name and characteristics are taken from the goat is related to Dionysus himself. Almost everywhere, the central point of these celebrations consisted of an exuberant sexual promiscuity, whose waves flooded over all established family practices and traditional laws. The wildest bestiality of nature was here unleashed, creating an abominable mixture of lust and cruelty, which has always seemed to me the real witches' potion.

From the feverish excitement of these festivals, knowledge of which reached the Greeks from all directions, by land and sea, they were apparently for a long time completely secure and protected through the figure of Apollo, drawn up in all his pride. Apollo could counter by holding up the head of Medusa in the face of the unequalled power of this crude and grotesque Dionysian force. Doric art has immortalized this majestic bearing of Apollo as he stands in opposition. This opposition became more dubious and even impossible as similar impulses gradually broke out from the deepest roots of Hellenic culture itself. Now the effect of the Delphic god, in a timely process of reconciliation, limited itself to taking the destructive weapon out of the hand of his powerful opponent.

This reconciliation is the most important moment in the history of Greek culture. Wherever we look the revolutionary effects of this experience manifest themselves. It was the reconciliation of two opponents, who from now on observed their differences with a sharp demarcation of the border line between them and with occasional gifts send to honour each other. Basically the gap was not bridged over. However, if we see how, under the pressure of this peace agreement, the Dionysian power revealed itself, then we now understand the meaning of the festivals of world redemption and days of transfiguration in the Dionysian orgies of the Greeks, in comparison with the Babylonian Sacaea, which turned human beings back into tigers and apes.

In these Greek festivals, for the first time nature achieves its artistic jubilee. In them, for the first time, the tearing apart of the principii individuationis [the individualizing principle] becomes an artistic phenomenon. Here that dreadful witches' potion of lust and cruelty was without power. The strange mixture and ambiguity in the emotions of the Dionysian celebrant remind him, as healing potions remind him of deadly poison, of that sense that pain awakens joy, that the jubilation in his chest rips out cries of agony. From the most sublime joy echoes the cry of horror or the longingly plaintive lament over an irreparable loss. In those Greek festivals it was as if a sentimental feature of nature is breaking out, as if nature has to sigh over her dismemberment into separate individuals.

The language of song and poetry of such a doubly defined celebrant was for the Homeric Greek world something new and unheard of. Dionysian music especially awoke in that world fear and terror. If music was apparently already known as an Apollonian art, this music, strictly speaking, was a rhythmic pattern like the sound of waves, whose artistic power had developed for presenting Apollonian states of mind. The music of Apollo was Doric architecture expressed in sound, but only in intimate tones, characteristic of the cithara [a traditional stringed instrument]. The un-Apollonian character of Dionysian music keeps such an element of gentle caution at a distance, and with that turns music generally into emotionally disturbing tonal power, a unified stream of melody, and the totally incomparable world of harmony.

In the Dionysian dithyramb man is aroused to the highest intensity of all his symbolic capabilities. Something never felt before forces itself into expression—the destruction of the veil of Maja, the sense of oneness as the presiding genius of form, of nature itself. Now the essence of nature must express itself symbolically; a new world of symbols is necessary, the entire symbolism of the body, not just the symbolism of mouth, face, and words, but the full gestures of the dance—all the limbs moving to the rhythm. And then the other symbolic powers grow, those of music, rhythm, dynamics, and harmony—all with sudden spontaneity.

To grasp this total unleashing of all symbolic powers, man must already have attained that high level of freedom from the self which seeks to express itself symbolically in those forces. Because of this, the dithyrambic servant of Dionysus will understand only someone like himself. With what astonishment must the Apollonian Greek have gazed at him! With an amazement which was all the greater as he sensed with horror that all this may not be really foreign to him, that even his Apollonian consciousness was covering the Dionysian world in front of him, like a veil.

3

In order to grasp this point, we must dismantle that artistic structure of Apollonian culture, as it were, stone by stone, until we see the foundations on which it is built. Here we become aware for the first time of the marvelous Olympian divine forms, which stand on the pediments of this building and whose actions decorate its friezes all around in illuminating bas relief. If Apollo also stands among them, as a single god next to the others and without any claim to the pre-eminent position, we should not on that account let ourselves be deceived. The same instinct which made Apollo perceptible to the senses gave birth to the entire Olympian world in general. In this sense, we must value Apollo as the father of them all. What was the immense need out of which such an illuminating group of Olympic beings arose?

Anyone who steps up to these Olympians with another religion in his heart and seeks from them ethical loftiness, even sanctity or spiritual longing for the non-physical, for loving gazes filled with pity, must soon enough despondently turn his back on them in disappointment. For here there is no reminder of asceticism, spirituality, and duty. Here speaks to us only a full, indeed a triumphant, existence, in which everything present is worshipped, no matter whether it is good or evil. And thus the onlooker may well stand in real consternation in front of this fantastic excess of life, to ask himself with what magical drink in their bodies these high-spirited men could have enjoyed life so that wherever they look, Helen laughs back at them, that ideal image of their own existence, "hovering in sweet sensuousness.".

However, we must summon back this onlooker who has already turned around to go away. "Don't leave them. First listen to what Greek folk wisdom expresses about this very life which spreads out before you here with such inexplicable serenity. There is an old saying to the effect that King Midas for a long time hunted the wise Silenus, the companion of Dionysus, in the forests, without catching him. When Silenus finally fell into the king's hands, the king asked what was the best thing of all for men, the very finest. The daemon remained silent, motionless and inflexible, until, compelled by the king, he finally broke out into shrill laughter and said, 'Suffering creature, born for a day, child of accident and toil, why are you forcing me to say what is the most unpleasant thing for you to hear? The very best thing for you is totally unreachable: not to have been born, not to exist, to be nothing. The second best thing for you, however, is this: to die soon.'"

What is the relationship between the Olympian world of the gods and this popular wisdom? It is like the relationship of the entrancing vision of the tortured martyr to his pain.

Now, as it were, the Olympic magic mountain reveals itself to us and shows us its roots. The Greek knew and felt the terror and horror of existence. In order to live at all, he must have placed in front of him the gleaming Olympians, born in his dreams. That immense distrust of the titanic forces of nature, that Moira [Fate] enthroned mercilessly above all knowledge, that vulture that devoured Prometheus, friend of man, that fatal lot drawn by wise Oedipus, that family curse on the House of Atreus, that Orestes compelled to kill his mother, in short, that entire philosophy of the woodland god, together with its mythical illustrations, from which the melancholy Etruscans died off, all that was overcome time after time by the Greeks (or at least hidden and removed from view) through the artistic middle world of the Olympians

In order to be able to live, the Greeks must have created these gods out of the deepest necessity. We can readily imagine the sequential development of these gods: through that instinctive Apollonian drive for beauty there developed by slow degrees out of the primordial titanic divine order of terror the Olympian divine order of joy, just as roses break forth out of thorny bushes. How else could a people so emotionally sensitive, so spontaneously desiring, so singularly capable of suffering have endured their existence, unless the same qualities manifested themselves in their gods, around whom flowed a higher glory. The same instinctual drive which summons art into life as the seductive replenishment for further living and the completion of existence also gave rise to the Olympian world, by which the Hellenic "Will" held before itself a transfiguring mirror.

In this way the gods justify the lives of men because they themselves live it—that is the only satisfactory theodicy! Existence under the bright sunshine of such gods is experienced as worth striving for in itself, and the essential pain of the Homeric men consists in the separation from that sunlight, above all in the fact that such separation is close at hand., so that we could say of them, with a reversal of the wisdom of Silenus, "the very worst thing for them was to die soon, the second worst was to die at all." When the laments resound now, they tell of short-lived Achilles, of the changes in the race of men, transformed like leaves, of the destruction of the heroic age. It is not unworthy of the greatest heroes to long to live on, even as a day labourer. In the Apollonian stage, the "Will" so spontaneously demands to live on, the Homeric man fills himself with that feeling so much, that even his lament becomes a song of praise.

At this point we must point out that this harmony, this union of man with nature (something looked on enviously by more recent ages), for which Schiller coined the artistic slogan "naïve," is in no way such a simple, inevitable, and, as it were, unavoidable condition (like a human paradise) which we necessarily run into at the door of every culture. Such a belief is possible only in an age which seeks to believe that Rousseau's Emile is an artist and imagines it has found in Homer an artist like Emile raised in the bosom of nature. Wherever we encounter the "naïve" in art, we have to recognize the highest effect of Apollonian culture, something which always must come into existence to overthrow the kingdom of the Titans, to kill monsters, and through powerfully deluding images and joyful illusions to emerge victorious over the horrific depths of what we observe in the world and the most sensitive capacity for suffering. But how seldom does the naïve, that sense of being completely swallowed up in the beauty of appearance, succeed. For that reason, how inexpressibly noble is Homer, who, as a single person, was related to Apollonian popular culture as the single dream artist to his people's capacity to dream and to nature in general.

Homeric "naïveté" is only to be understood as the complete victory of the Apollonian illusion. It is the sort of illusion which nature uses so frequently in order to attain her objectives. The true goal is concealed by a deluding image. We stretch our hands out toward this image, and nature reaches its goal through the deception. With the Greeks it was a case of the "Will" wishing to gaze upon itself through the transforming power of genius and the world of art. In order to celebrate itself, its creatures had to sense that they were worthy of being glorified—they must see themselves again in a higher sphere, without this complete world of contemplation affecting them as an imperative or as a reproach. This is the sphere of beauty, in which they saw their mirror images, the Olympians. With this mirror of beauty, the Hellenic "Will" fought against the talent for suffering and the wisdom of suffering which is bound up with artistic talent, and as a memorial of its victory Homer, the naïve artist, stands before us.

4

Using the analogy of a dream we can learn something about this naïve artist. If we recall how the dreamer, in the middle of his illusory dream world, calls out to himself, without destroying that world, "It is a dream. I want to continue dreaming," and if we can infer, on the one hand, a deep inner delight at the contemplation of dreams, and, on the other, that he must have completely forgotten the pressing problems of his daily life, in order to be capable of dreaming at all with such an inner contemplative joy, then we may interpret all these phenomena, with the guidance of Apollo, the interpreter of dreams, in something like the manner which follows below.

To be sure, with respect to both halves of life, the waking and the dreaming states, the first one strikes us as disproportionately better, more important, more valuable, more worth living—the only way to live. Nevertheless I can assert (something of a paradox to all appearances) on the basis of the secret foundation of our essence, whose manifestation we are, precisely the opposite evaluation of dreams. For the more I become aware of those all-powerful natural artistic impulses and the fervent yearning for illusion contained in them, the desire to be redeemed through appearances, the more I feel myself forced to the metaphysical assumption that the true basis of being , the ever suffering and entirely contradictory primordial oneness, constantly uses the delightful vision, the joyful illusion, to redeem itself. We are compelled to experience this illusion, totally caught up in it and constituted by it, as the truly non-existent, that is, as a continuing development in time, space, and causality, in other words, as an empirical reality. But if we momentarily look away from our own "reality, " if we grasp our empirical existence and the world in general as an idea of the primordial oneness created in each moment, then we must consider our dreams as illusions of illusions, as well as an even higher fulfillment of the primordial hunger for illusion. For the same reasons, the innermost core of nature takes an indescribable joy in the naïve artist and naïve works of art, which is, in the same way, only "an illusion of an illusion."

Rafael, himself one of those immortal "naïve" artists, in one of his allegorical paintings, has presented that issue of transforming an illusion into an illusion, the fundamental process of the naïve artist and Apollonian culture as well. In his Transfiguration the bottom half shows us, in the possessed boy, the despairing porters, and the helplessly frightened disciples, the mirror image of the eternal primordial pain, the sole basis of the world. The "illusion" here is the reflection of the eternal contradiction, the father of things. Now, out of this illusion there rises up, like an ambrosial fragrance, a new world of illusion, like a vision, invisible to those trapped in the first scene, something illuminating and hovering in the purest painless ecstasy, a shining vision to contemplate with eyes wide open.

Here we have before our very eyes in the highest symbolism of art that Apollonian world of beauty and its foundation, the frightening wisdom of Silenus, and we understand, through intuition, the reciprocal necessity for both of them. But Apollo confronts us once again as the divine manifestation of the principii individuationis [the individualizing principle], in which the eternally attained goal of the primordial oneness, its redemption through illusion, comes into being. He shows us, with his awe-inspiring gestures, how the entire world of torment is necessary, so that through it the individual is pushed to create the redemptive vision and then, absorbed in contemplation of that vision, sits quietly in his rowboat, tossing around in the middle of the ocean.

This deification of the principle of individualization, if it is thought of in general as commanding and proscriptive, understands only one law, that of the individual, that is, observing the limits of individualization, moderation in the Greek sense. Apollo, as the ethical divinity, demands moderation from his followers and self-knowledge, so that they can observe moderation.. And so alongside the aesthetic necessity of beauty run the demands "Know thyself" and "Nothing in excess." Arrogance and excess are considered the essentially hostile daemons of the non-Apollonian sphere, therefore characteristic of the pre-Apollonian period, the age of the Titans, and of the world beyond the Apollonian, that is, the barbarian world. Because of his Titanic love for mankind Prometheus had to be ripped apart by the vulture. For the sake of his excessive wisdom, which solved the riddle of the sphinx, Oedipus had to be overthrown in a bewildering whirlpool of evil. That is how the Delphic god interpreted the Greek past.

To the Apollonian Greeks the effect aroused by the Dionysian also seemed "Titanic" and "barbaric." But they could not, with that response, conceal that they themselves were, nonetheless, internally related and similar to those deposed Titans and heroes. Indeed, they must have felt even more that their entire existence, with all its beauty and moderation, rested on some hidden underground of suffering and knowledge which was reawakened through that very Dionysian. And look! Apollo could not live without Dionysus! The "Titanic" and the "barbaric" were, in the end, every bit as necessary as the Apollonian.

And now let us imagine how in this world, constructed on illusion and moderation and restrained by art, the ecstatic sound of the Dionysian celebration rang out all around with a constantly tempting magic, how in such celebrations the entire excess of nature sang out loudly in joy, suffering, and knowledge, even in the most piercing scream. Let's imagine what the psalm-chanting Apollonian artist, with his ghostly harp music could offer in comparison to this daemonic popular singing. The muses of the art of "illusion" withered away in the face of an art which spoke truth in its intoxicated state: the wisdom of Silenus cried out "Woe! Woe!" against the serene Olympian. Individualism, with all its limits and moderation, was destroyed in the self-forgetfulness of the Dionysian condition and forgot its Apollonian principles.

Excess revealed itself as the truth. The contradictory ecstasy born from of pain spoke of itself right out of the heart of nature. And so the Apollonian was canceled and destroyed, above all where the Dionysian penetrated. But it is just as certain that in those places where the first onslaught was halted, the high reputation and the majesty of the Delphic god manifested itself more firmly and threateningly than ever. For I can explain the Doric state and Doric art only as a constant Apollonian war camp. Only through an uninterrupted opposition to the Titanic-barbaric essence of the Dionysian could such a defiantly aloof art, protected on all sides with fortifications, such a harsh upbringing as a preparation for war, and such a cruel and ruthless basis for government endure.

Up to this point I have set out at some length what I observed at the opening of this essay: how the Dionysian and the Apollonian ruled the Hellenic world, in a constant sequence of births, one after the other, mutually intensifying each other, how, out of the "first" ages, with their battles of the Titans and their harsh popular philosophy, the Homeric world developed under the rule of the Apollonian drive for beauty, how this "naïve" magnificence is swallowed up once more by the breaking out of the Dionysian torrent, and how in opposition to this new power the Apollonian erected the rigid majesty of Doric art and the Doric world view.

If in this way the ancient history of the Greeks, in the struggle of these two hostile principles, falls into four major artistic periods, we are now impelled to ask more about the final stage of this development and striving, in case we should consider the last attained period, the one of Doric art, as the summit and intention of these artistic impulses. Here, the lofty and highly much praised artistic achievement of Attic tragedy and the dramatic dithyramb presents itself before our eyes, as the common goal of both artistic drives, whose secret marriage partnership, after a long antecedent struggle, celebrated itself with such a child, simultaneously Antigone and Cassandra.

5

We are now approaching the essential goal of our undertaking, which aims at a knowledge of the Dionysian-Apollonian genius and its works of art, or at least an intuitive understanding of its mysterious unity. Here now we raise the question of where that new seed first appears in the Hellenic world, the seed which later develops into tragedy and the dramatic dithyramb. On this question classical antiquity itself gives us illustrative evidence when it places Homer and Archilochus next to each other as the originators and torch-bearers of Greek poetry in paintings, cameos, and so on, in full confidence that only these two should be considered equally the original natures from whom a fire-storm flowed out over the entire later world of the Greeks.

Homer, the ancient self-absorbed dreamer, the archetype of the naïve Apollonian artist, now stares astonished at the passionate head of wild Archilochus, the fighting servant of the muses, battered by existence. In its interpretative efforts, our recent aesthetics has known only how to indicate that here the first "subjective" artist stands in contrast to the "objective" artist. This interpretation is of little use, since we recognize the subjective artist as a bad artist and demand in every art and every high artistic achievement, first and foremost, a victory over the subjective, redemption from the "I," and the silence of every individual will and desire—indeed, we are incapable of accepting the slightest artistic creation as true, unless it has objectivity and a purely disinterested contemplation.

Hence, our aesthetic must first solve the problem of how it is possible for the "lyricist" to be an artist. For he, according to the experience of all ages, always says "I" and sings out the entire chromatic sequence of the sounds of his passions and desires. This Archilochus immediately startles us, alongside Homer, through his cry of hate and scorn, through the drunken eruptions of his desire. By doing this, isn't Archilochus (the first artist called subjective) essentially a non-artist?

But then where does that veneration come from, which the Delphic oracle, the centre of "objective" art, showed to him, the poet, in very remarkable sayings.

Schiller has illuminated his own writing process with a psychological observation, inexplicable to him, which nevertheless does not appear questionable. He confesses that when he was in a state of preparation, before he actually started writing, he did not have something like a series of pictures, with a structured causality of ideas, in front of him, but rather a musical mood: "With me, feeling at first lacks a defined and clear object—that develops for the first time later on. A certain musical emotional state comes first, and from this, with me, the poetic idea then follows."

Now, if we add the most important phenomenon of the entire ancient lyric, the union, universally acknowledged as natural, between the lyricist and the musician, even their common identity (in comparison with which our recent lyrics look like the image of a god without a head) then we can, on the basis of the aesthetic metaphysics we established earlier, account for the lyric poet in the following manner. He has, first of all, as a Dionysian artist, become entirely one with the primordial oneness of his painful contradictory nature and produces the reflection of this primordial oneness as music, if music can with justice be called a re-working of the world, its second coat. But now this music becomes perceptible to him once again, as in a metaphorical dream image, under the influence of Apollonian dreaming. That reflection, which lacks imagery and concepts, of the original pain in music, together with its redemption in illusion, gives rise now to a second reflection as the particular metaphor or illustration. The artist has already surrendered his subjectivity in the Dionysian process. The image which now reveals his unity with the heart of the world is a dream scene, which symbolizes that original contradiction and pain, together with the primordial joy in illusion. The "I" of the lyric poet thus echoes out of the abyss of being. What recent aestheticians mean by his "subjectivity" is mere fantasy.

When Archilochus, the first Greek lyric poet, announces his raging love and, at the same time, his contempt for the daughters of Lycambes, it is not his own passion which dances in front of us in an orgiastic frenzy. We see Dionysus and the maenads; we see the intoxicated reveler Archilochus sunk down in sleep—as Euripides describes in the Bacchae, asleep in a high Alpine meadow in the midday sun—and now Apollo steps up to him and touches him with his laurel. The Dionysian musical enchantment of the sleeper now, as it were, flashes around him fiery images, lyrical poems, which are called, in their highest form, tragedies and dramatic dithyrambs.

The plastic artist as well as his relation, the epic poet, is absorbed in the pure contemplation of images. The Dionysian musician lacks any image and is in himself only and entirely the original pain and original reverberation of that image. The lyrical genius feels a world of images and metaphors grow up out of the mysteriously unified state of renunciation of the self. These have a colour, causality, and speed entirely different from that world of the plastic artist and the writer of epic. While the last of these (the epic poet) lives in these pictures and only in them with joyful contentment and does not get tired of contemplating them with love, right down to the smallest details. Even the image of the angry Achilles is for him only a picture whose expressions of anger he enjoys with that dream joy in illusions, so that he, by this mirror of appearances, is protected against the development of that sense of unity and being fused together with the forms he has created. By contrast, the images of the lyric poet are nothing but himself and, as it were, only different objectifications of himself. He can say "I" because he is the moving central point of that world. Only this "I" is not the same as the "I" of the awake, empirically real man, but the single "I" of true and eternal being in general, the "I" resting on the foundation of things. Through its portrayal the lyrical genius sees right into the very basis of things.

Now let's imagine how he looks upon himself among these likenesses, as a non-genius, that is, as his own "Subject," the entire unruly crowd of subjective passions and striving of his will aiming at something particular, which seems real to him. If it now seems as if the lyrical genius and the non-genius bound up with him were one and the same and as if he first spoke that little word "I" about himself, then this illusion could no longer deceive us, not at least in the way it deceived those who have defined the lyricist as a subjective poet.

To tell the truth, Archilochus, the man of passionately burning love and hate, is only a vision of the genius who is no longer Archilochus any more but a world genius and who expresses his primordial pain symbolically in Archilochus as a metaphor for man. That subjectively willing and desiring man Archilochus can never ever be a poet. It is not at all essential that the lyric poet see directly in front of him the phenomenon of the man Archilochus as a reflection of eternal being. Tragedy shows how far the visionary world of the lyric poet can distance itself from that phenomenon clearly standing near at hand.

Schopenhauer, who did not hide from the difficulty which the lyric poet creates for the philosophical observer of art, believed that he had discovered a solution (something which I cannot go along with) when in his profound metaphysics of music he found a way setting the difficulty decisively to one side, as I believe I have done in his spirit and with due honour to him. He describes the essential nature of song as follows:.

The consciousness of the singer is filled with the subject of willing, that is, his own willing, often as an unleashed satisfied willing (joy), but also, and more often, as a restricted willing (sorrow). It is always a mobile condition of the heart: emotional and passionate. However, alongside this condition, the singer simultaneously, through a glimpse at the surrounding nature, becomes aware of himself as a subject of the pure, will-less knowledge, whose imperturbable, blessed tranquilly now enters to contrast the pressure of his always dull, always still limited willing. The sensation of this contrast, this game back and forth, is basically what expresses itself in the totality of the song and what, in general, creates the lyrical state. In this state, pure understanding, as it were, comes to us, to save us from willing and the pressures of willing. We follow along, but only moment by moment. The will, the memory of our personal goals, constantly interrupts this calm contemplation of ours, over and over again, but the next beautiful setting, in which pure will-less knowledge presents itself to us, always, once again, releases us from willing. Hence, in the song and the lyrical mood, willing (our personal interest in our own purposes) and pure contemplation in the setting which presents itself are miraculously mixed up together. We seek and imagine relationships between them both. The subjective mood, the emotional state of the will, communicates with the surroundings we contemplate, and the latter, in turn, gives its colour to our mood, in a reflex action. The true song is the expression of this entire emotional condition, mixed and divided in this way." (World as Will and Idea, I, 295)

Who can fail to recognize in this description that here the lyric has been characterized as an incompletely realized art, a leap, as it were, which seldom attains its goal, indeed, as a semi-art, whose essence must consist of the fact that the will and pure contemplation, that is, the unaesthetic and the aesthetic conditions, must be miraculously mixed up together? In contrast to this, we maintain that the entire opposition, which even Schopenhauer uses as a measurement of value to classify art, that opposition of the subjective and the objective, has generally no place in aesthetics, since the subject, the willing individual demanding his own egotistical purposes, can only be thought of as an enemy of art not as its origin.

But insofar as the subject is an artist, he is already released from his individual willing and has become, so to speak, a medium through which a subject of true being celebrates its redemption. For we need to be clear on this point, above everything else (to our humiliation or ennoblement): the entire comedy of art does not present itself for us in order to make us better or to educate us—even less so that we should be the true creators of the art world. We should really look upon ourselves as beautiful pictures and artistic projections of the true creator, and in that significance as works of art we have our highest value, for only as an aesthetic phenomena are existence and the world eternally justified, while, of course, our own consciousness of this significance of ours is no different from the consciousness which soldiers painted on canvas have of the battle portrayed there.

Hence our entire knowledge of art is basically completely illusory, because, as knowing people, we are not one with or identical to that being who, as the single creator and spectator of that comedy of art, prepares for itself an eternal enjoyment. Only to the extent that the genius in the act of artistic creation is fused with that primordial artist of the world, does he know anything about the eternal nature of art, only in that state in which (as in the weird picture of fairy tales) he can miraculously turn his eyes and contemplate himself. Now he is simultaneously subject and object, all at once poet, actor, and spectator.

6

With respect to Archilochus, learned scholarship has revealed that he introduced the folk song into literature and that, because of this achievement, he earned his place next to Homer in the universal estimation of the Greeks. But what is the folk song in comparison to the completely Apollonian epic poem? What else but the perpetuum vestigum [the eternal mark] of a union between the Apollonian and the Dionysian? Its tremendous expansion, extending to all peoples and constantly increasing with new births, testifies to us how strong that artistic duality of nature is: which, to use an analogy, leaves its trace behind in the folk song just as the orgiastic movements of a people leave their traces in its music. Indeed, it must also be historically demonstrable how that period rich in folk songs at the same time was stirred in the strongest manner by Dionysian trends, something which we have to recognize as the foundation and precondition of folk songs.

But to begin with, we must view the folk song as the musical mirror of the world, as the primordial melody, which seeks for a parallel dream image of itself and expresses this in poetry. The melody is thus primary and universal, for which reason it can undergo many objectifications, in several texts. It is also far more important and more essential in the naïve evaluations of the people. Melody gives birth to poetry from itself, over and over again. The forms of the strophes in the folk song indicate that to us. I have always observed this phenomenon with astonishment, until I finally came up with this explanation. Whoever looks at a collection of folk songs, for example, Des Knaben Wunderhorn [The Boy's Miraculous Horn] with this theory in mind will find countless examples of how the continually fecund melody emits fiery showers of images all around. These images, with their bright colours, sudden alteration, and their wild momentum, reveal a power completely foreign to the epic illusion and its calm forward progress. From the standpoint of epic this uneven and irregular word of images in the lyric is easy to condemn—something no doubt the solemn rhapsodists of the Apollonian celebrations did in the age of Terpander.

Thus, in the poetry of the folk song we see the language of poetry most strongly pressured to imitate music. Hence, with Archilochus a new world of poetry begins, something which conflicts very profoundly with the Homeric world. Here we have demonstrated the one possible relationship between poetry and music, word and tone: word, image, and idea look for metaphorical expression in music and experience the power of music. In this sense we can distinguish two main streams in the history of the language of the Greek people: language which imitates appearance and images and language which imitates the world of music.

Let's think for a moment more deeply about the linguistic difference in colour, syntactic structure, and vocabulary between Homer and Pindar in order to grasp the significance of this contrast. It will become crystal clear to some that between Homer and Pindar the orgiastic flute melodies of Olympus must have rung out, music which even in the time of Aristotle, in the midst of an infinitely more sophisticated music, drove people into raptures of drunken enthusiasm and with their natural effects no doubt stimulated all the poetical forms of expression of contemporaries to imitate them.

I recall here a well-known phenomenon of our own times, something which strikes our aestheticians as objectionable. Again and again we experience how a Beethoven symphony makes it necessary for the individual listener to talk in images, even if it's true that the collection of different worlds of imagery created by a musical piece really looks fantastically confused, even contradictory. The most proper style of our aestheticians is to exercise their lame wits on such a collection and to overlook the phenomenon which is really worth explaining. Even when the tone poet has spoken in images about his composition, for example, when he describes a symphony as a pastoral, one movement as "A Scene by the Brook," and another as "A Frolicking Meeting of Peasants," these expressions are in any event only metaphors, images born out of the music and not some objective condition imitated by the music. These notions cannot teach us anything at all about the Dionysian content of the music and have no exclusive value alongside other pictures.

Now, we have only to transfer this process of unloading music into pictures to a large, youthful, linguistically creative population in order to sense how the strophic folk song arose and how the entire linguistic capability was stimulated by a new principle, the imitation of music. If we can thus consider the lyrical poem as the mimetic efflorescence of music in pictures and ideas, then we can now ask the following question: "What does music look like in the mirror of imagery and ideas?" It appears as the will, taking that word in Schopenhauer's sense, that is, as the opposite to the aesthetic, pure, contemplative, will-less state. Here we should differentiate as sharply as possible the idea of being from the idea of appearance. For it is impossible for music, given its nature, to be the will, because if that were the case we would have to ban music entirely from the realm of art. For the will consists of what is inherently unaesthetic. But music appears as the will.

In order to express that appearance in images, the lyric poet needs all the excitement of passion, from the whispers of affection right to the ravings of lunacy. Under the impulse to speak of music in Apollonian metaphors, he understands all nature and himself in nature only as eternal willing, desiring, yearning. However, insofar as he interprets music in images, he is resting in the still tranquility of the sea of Apollonian observation, no matter how much everything which he contemplates through that medium of music is moving around him, pushing and driving. Indeed, if he looks at himself through that same medium, his own image reveals itself to him in a condition of emotional dissatisfaction. His own willing, yearning, groaning, and cheering are for him a metaphor which he interprets the music for himself. This is the phenomenon of the lyric poet: as an Apollonian genius he interprets the music through the image of the will, while he himself, fully released from the greed of his will, is a pure, untroubled eye of the sun.

This entire discussion firmly maintains that the lyric is just as dependent on the spirit of music as is music itself. In its complete freedom, music does not use image and idea, but only tolerates them as something additional to itself. The poetry of the lyricist can express nothing which was not already latent in the immense universality and validity of the music, which forces him to speak in images. The world symbolism of music for this very reason cannot in any way be overcome by or reduced to language, because music addresses itself symbolically to the primordial contradiction and pain in the heart of the original oneness, and thus presents in symbolic form a sphere which is above all appearances and prior to them. In comparison with music, each appearance is far more a mere metaphor. Hence, language, the organ and symbol of appearances, never ever converts the deepest core of music to something external, but always remains, as long as it involves itself with the imitation of music, only in superficial contact with the music. The full eloquence of lyric poetry cannot bring us one step closer to the deepest meaning of music.

7

We must now seek assistance from all the artistic principles laid out above in order to find our way correctly through the labyrinth—a descriptive term we have to use to designate the origin of Greek tragedy. I don't think I'm saying anything illogical when I claim that the problem of this origin has not once been seriously formulated up to now, let alone solved, no matter how frequently the scattered scraps of ancient tradition have been put together in combinations with one another and then again ripped apart.

This tradition tells us very emphatically that tragedy developed out of the tragic chorus and originally consisted only of a chorus and nothing else. This fact requires us to look into the heart of this tragic chorus as the essential original drama, without allowing ourselves to be satisfied in any way with the common styles of talking about art—that the chorus is the ideal spectator or had the job of standing in for the people over against the royal area of the scene.

That last mentioned point, a conceptual explanation which sounds so lofty for many politicians (as though the invariable moral law was presented by the democratic Athenians in the people's chorus, which was always proved right in matters dealing with their kings' passionate acts of violence and excess) may have been suggested by a word from Aristotle. But such an idea has no influence on the original formation of tragedy, since all the opposition between people and ruler and every political-social issue in general is excluded from those purely religious origins. Looking with hindsight back on the classical form of the chorus known to us in Aeschylus and Sophocles we might well consider it blasphemous to talk of a premonition of the "constitutional popular representation" here. Others, however, have not been deterred from this blasphemous assertion. The ancient political organizations had no practical knowledge of a constitutional popular representation and they never once "had a hopeful premonition" of such things in their tragedies.

Much more famous than this political explanation of the chorus is A. W. Schlegel's idea. He recommended that we consider the chorus to some extent as a sample embodiment of the crowd of onlookers, as the "ideal spectator." This view, combined with that historical tradition that originally the tragedy consisted entirely of the chorus, reveals itself for what it is, a crude and unscholarly, although dazzling, claim. But the glitter survives only in the compact form of the expression, from the real German prejudice for everything which is called "ideal," and from our momentary astonishment.

For we are astonished, as soon as we compare the theatre public we know well with that chorus and ask ourselves whether it would be at all possible on the basis of this public to derive some idealization analogous to the tragic chorus. We silently deny this and then are surprised by the audacity of Schlegel's claim as well as by the totally different nature of the Greek general public. For we had always thought that the proper spectator, whoever he might be, must always remain conscious that he has a work of art in front of him, not an empirical reality. By contrast, the tragic chorus of the Greeks is required to recognize the shapes on the stage as living, existing people. The chorus of Oceanids really believes that they see the Titan Prometheus in front of them and consider themselves every bit as real as the god of the scene.

And is that supposed to be the highest and purest type of spectator, a person who, like the Oceanids, considers Prometheus vitally alive and real? Would it be a mark of the ideal spectator to run up onto the stage and free the god from his torment? We had believed in an aesthetic public and considered the individual spectator sufficiently capable, the more he was in a position to take the work of art as art, that is, aesthetically. This saying of Schlegel's indicates to us that the completely ideal spectator lets the scenic world work on him, not aesthetically at all, but vitally and empirically. "Oh, what about these Greeks!" we sigh, "they are knocking over our aesthetics!" But once we get used to that idea, we repeat Schlegel's saying every time we talk about the chorus.

But that emphatic tradition speaks here against Schlegel. The chorus in itself, without the stage, that is, the primitive form of tragedy, and that chorus of ideal spectators are not compatible. What sort of artistic style would we have if from this the idea of the spectator we derived, as its essential form, the "spectator in himself" (the pure spectator). The spectator without a play is a contradictory idea. We suspect that the birth of tragedy cannot be explained either from the high estimation of the moral intelligence of the masses or from the idea of the spectator without a play. And we consider this problem too profound to be touched by such superficial styles of commentary.

Schiller has already provided an infinitely more valuable insight into the meaning of the chorus in the famous preface to the Bride from Messina—the chorus viewed as a living wall which tragedy draws about itself in order to separate itself cleanly from the real world and to protect its ideal space and its poetical freedom for itself. With this as his main weapon Schiller fought against the common idea of naturalism, against the common demand for illusionistic dramatic poetry. While in the theatre daytime might be only artistic and stage architecture only symbolic, and the nature of the metrical language might have an ideal quality, nevertheless, on the whole, a misconception still ruled: it was not enough, Schiller claimed, that people merely tolerated as poetic freedom what was the essence of all poetry. The introduction of the chorus, according to Schiller, was the decisive step with which war was declared openly and nobly against naturalism in art.

Such a way of looking at things is the one, it strikes me, for which our age (which considers itself so superior) uses the dismissive catch phrase "pseudo-idealism." I suspect, by contrast, that with our present worship of naturalism and realism we are situated at the opposite pole from all idealism, namely, in the region of a wax works collection. In that, too, there is an art, as in certain romance novels of the present time. Only let no one pester us with the claim that with this we have overthrown the artistic "pseudo-idealism" of Schiller and Goethe.

Of course, it is an "ideal" stage on which, following Schiller's correct insight, the Greek satyr chorus, the chorus of the primitive tragedy, customarily strolled, a stage lifted high above over the real strolling stage of mortal men. For this chorus the Greeks constructed a suspended hovering framework of an imaginary natural condition and on it placed imaginary natural beings. Tragedy grew up out of this foundation and, for that very reason, has, from its inception, been spared the embarrassing business of counterfeiting reality.

That is not to say that it is a world arbitrarily fantasized somewhere between heaven and earth. It is much rather a world possessing the same reality and credibility for the devout Greek as the world of Olympus, together with its inhabitants. The satyr as the Dionysian chorus member lives in a reality permitted by religion, sanctioned by myth and culture. The fact that tragedy begins with him, that out of him the Dionysian wisdom of tragedy speaks, is a phenomenon as foreign to us here as the development of tragedy out of the chorus generally.

Perhaps we can reach a starting point for this discussion when I offer the claim that the satyr himself, the imaginary natural being, is related to the cultural person in the same way that Dionysian music is related to civilization. On this last point Richard Wagner states that civilization is neutralized by music in the same way lamplight is by daylight. In just such a manner, I believe, the cultured Greek felt himself neutralized by the sight of the chorus of satyrs. This is the most direct effect of Dionysian tragedy: generally , the state and society, the gap between man and man give way to an invincible feeling of unity which leads back to the heart of nature.

The metaphysical consolation, which as I have already indicated, true tragedy leaves us, that at the bottom of everything, in spite of all the transformations in phenomena, life is indestructibly power and delightful, this consolation appears in lively clarity as the chorus of satyrs, the chorus of natural beings, who live, as it were, behind civilization, who cannot disappear, and who, in spite of all the changes in generations and a people's history, always remain the same. With this chorus, the profound Greek, capable of the most delicate and the most severe suffering, consoled himself, the man who looked around with a daring gaze in the middle of the terrifying destructive instincts of so-called world history and equally into the cruelty of nature and who is in danger of longing for the denial of the will of Buddhism. Art saves him, and through art life saves him.

The ecstasy of the Dionysian state, with its destruction of the customary manacles and boundaries of existence, contains, of course, for as long as it lasts a lethargic element, in which everything personally experienced in the past is immersed. Through this gulf of oblivion, the world of everyday reality and the Dionysian reality separate from each other. As soon as that daily reality comes back again into consciousness, one feels it as something disgusting. The fruit of this condition is an ascetic condition, in which one denies the power of the will.

In this sense the Dionysian man has similarities to Hamlet. Both have had a real glimpse into the essence of things. They have understood, and it now disgusts them to act, for their actions can change nothing in the eternal nature of things. They perceive as ridiculous or humiliating the fact that it is expected of them that they should set right a world turned upside down. The knowledge kills action, for action requires a state of being in which we are covered with the veil of illusion. That is what Hamlet has to teach us, not that really venal wisdom about John-a-Dreams, who cannot move himself to act because of too much reflection, too many possibilities, so to speak. It's not a case of reflection. No! The true knowledge, the glimpse into the cruel truth overcomes the driving motive to act, both in Hamlet as well as in the Dionysian man.

Now no consolation has any effect. His longing goes out over the world, even beyond the gods themselves, toward death. Existence is denied, together with its blazing reflection in the gods or an immortal afterlife. In the consciousness of once having glimpsed the truth, man now sees everywhere only the horror or absurdity of being; now he understands the symbolism in the fate of Ophelia; now he recognizes the wisdom of the forest god Silenus. It disgusts him.

Here the will is in the highest danger. Thus, to be saved, it comes close to the healing magician, art. Art alone can turn those thoughts of disgust at the horror or absurdity of existence into imaginary constructs, which permit living to continue. These constructs are the Sublime as the artistic mastering of the horrible and the Comic as the artistic release from disgust at the absurd. The chorus of satyrs in the dithyramb is the saving fact of Greek art. The emotional fits I have just described play themselves out by means of the world of these Dionysian attendants.

8

The satyr and the idyllic shepherd of our more recent times are both the epitome of a longing directed toward the primordial and natural, but with what a strong fearless grip the Greek held onto his men from the woods, and how timidly and weakly modern man toys with the flattering image of a delicate and gentle flute-playing shepherd! The Greek who had not been worked on as yet by any knowledge which kept culture imprisoned saw nature in his satyr, and so he did not yet mistake satyrs for apes. Quite the contrary: the satyr was the primordial image of man, the expression of his highest and strongest emotions, as an inspired reveler, enraptured by the approach of the god, as a sympathetic companion, in whom the suffering of the god was repeated, as a messenger bringing wisdom from the deepest heart of nature, as a perceptible image of the sexual omnipotence of nature, which the Greek was accustomed to observing with reverent astonishment.

The satyr was something sublime and divine—that's how he must have seemed especially to the painfully broken gaze of the Dionysian man, who would have been insulted by our well groomed fictitious shepherd. His eye lingered with sublime satisfaction on the exposed, vigorous, and magnificent script of nature. Here the illusion of culture was wiped away by the primordial image of man. Here the real man revealed himself, the bearded satyr who cried out with joy to his god. In comparison with him the man of culture was reduced to a misleading caricature. Schiller was also right to see in these matters the start of tragic art: the chorus is a living wall against the pounding reality, because it—the satyr chorus—presents existence more genuinely, truly, and completely than does the civilized person, who generally considers himself the only reality.

The sphere of poetry does not lie beyond this world as the fantastic impossibility of a poet's brain. It wants to be exactly the opposite, the unadorned expression of the truth, and it must therefore cast off the false costume of that truth thought up by the man of culture. The contrast of this real truth of nature and the cultural lie which behaves as if it is the only reality is similar to the contrast between the eternal core of things, the thing-in-itself, and the total world of appearances. And just as tragedy, with its metaphysical consolation, draws attention to the eternal life of that existential core in the continuing destruction of appearances, so the symbolism of the satyr chorus already expresses metaphorically that primordial relationship between the thing-in-itself and appearances. That idyllic shepherd of modern man is only a counterfeit, the totality of cultural illusions which he counts as nature. The Dionysian Greek wants truth and nature in their highest power: he seems himself transformed into a satyr.

The enraptured horde of those who served Dionysus rejoiced under the influence of such moods and insights, whose power transformed them before their very eyes, so that they imagined themselves as restored natural geniuses, as satyrs. The later constitution of the tragic chorus is the artistic imitation of that natural phenomenon, in which now a division was surely necessary between the Dionysian spectators and those under the Dionysian enchantment. But we must always remind ourselves that the public in Attic tragedy re-discovered itself in chorus of the orchestra and that basically there was no opposition between the public and the chorus. For everything is only a huge sublime chorus of dancing and singing satyrs or of those people who permit themselves to be represented by these satyrs.

We must now appropriate that saying of Schlegel's in a deeper sense. The chorus is the "ideal spectator," insofar as it is the only onlooker, the person who sees the visionary world of the scene. A public of spectators, as we know it, was unknown to the Greeks. In their theatre, given the way the spectators' space was built up in terraces, raised up in concentric rings, it was possible for everyone quite literally to look out over the collective cultural world around him and with a complete perspective to imagine himself a member of the chorus. Given this insight, we can call the chorus, in its primitive stages of the prototypical tragedy, the self-reflection of Dionysian men, a phenomenon which we can make out most clearly in the experience of the actor, who, if he is really gifted, sees perceptibly before his eyes the image of the role he has to play, hovering there for him to grasp.

The satyr chorus is, first and foremost, a vision of the Dionysian mass, just as, in turn, the world of the acting area is a vision of this satyr chorus. The power of this vision is strong enough to dull and desensitize the impression of "reality," the sight of the cultured people ranged in their rows of seats all around. The form of the Greek theatre is a reminder of a solitary mountain valley. The architecture of the scene appears as an illuminated picture of a cloud, which the Bacchae gaze upon, as they swarm down from the mountain heights, as the majestic setting in the middle of which the image of Dionysus is revealed.

This primitive artistic illusion, which we are putting into words here to explain the tragic chorus, is, from the perspective of our scholarly views about the basic artistic process, almost offensive, although nothing can be more obvious than that the poet is only a poet because of the fact that he sees himself surrounded by shapes which live and act in front of him and into whose innermost being he gazes. Through some peculiar weakness in our modern talent, we are inclined to imagine that primitive aesthetic phenomenon in too complicated and abstract a manner.

For the true poet, metaphor is not a rhetorical trope, but a representative image which really hovers in front of him in the place of an idea. The character is for him not a totality put together from individual traits collected bit by bit, but a living person, insistently there before his eyes, which differs from the similar vision of the painter only through its continued further living and acting. Why does Homer give us descriptions so much more vivid than all the poets? Because he sees so much more around him. We speak about poetry so abstractly because we all tend to be poor poets. The aesthetic phenomenon is fundamentally simple: if someone just possesses the capacity to see a living game going on and to live all the time surrounded by hordes of ghosts, then that man is a poet. If someone just feels the urge to change himself and to speak out from other bodies and souls, then that person is a dramatist.

Dionysian excitement is capable of communicating this artistic talent to an entire multitude, so that they see themselves surrounded by such a horde of ghosts with which they know they are innerly one. This dynamic of the tragic chorus is the original dramatic phenomenon: to see oneself transformed before one's eyes and now to act as if one really had entered another body, another character. This process stands right at the beginning of the development of drama. Here is something different from the rhapsodist, who never fuses with his images, but, like the painter, sees them with an observing eye outside himself. In this drama there is already a surrender of individuality by entering into a strange nature. And this phenomenon breaks out like an epidemic; an entire horde feels itself enchanted in this way.

For this reason the dithyramb is essentially different from every other choral song. The virgins who move solemnly to Apollo's temple with laurel branches in their hands singing a processional song as they go, remain who they are and retain their names as citizens. The dithyrambic chorus is a chorus of transformed people, for whom their civic past, their social position, is completely forgotten. They have become their god's timeless servants, living beyond all regions of society. All other choral lyrics of the Greeks are only an immense intensification of the Apollonian solo singer; whereas in the dithyramb a congregation of unconscious actors stands before us, who look upon each other as transformed. Enchantment is the precondition for all dramatic art. In this enchantment the Dionysian reveler sees himself as a satyr, and then, in turn, as a satyr he looks at his god. That is, in his transformed state he sees a new vision outside himself as an Apollonian fulfillment of his condition. With this new vision drama is complete.

With this knowledge in mind, we must understand Greek tragedy as the Dionysian chorus which over and over again constantly discharges itself in an Apollonian world of images. Those choral passages interspersed through tragedy are thus, as it were, the maternal bosom of the entire dialogue so-called, that is, of the totality of the stage word, the drama itself. This primordial basis of tragedy sends its vision pulsing out in several discharges following one after the other, a vision which is entirely a dream image and therefore epic in nature, but, on the other hand, as an objectification of a Dionysian state, it presents not the Apollonian consolation in illusion, but its opposite, the smashing of individuality and becoming one with primordial being. With this, drama is the Apollonian projection of Dionysian knowledge and effects, and thus is separated by an immense gulf from epic.

This conception of ours provides a full explanation for the chorus of Greek tragedy, the symbol for the total frenzied Dionysian multitude.

While, given what we are used to with the role of the chorus on the modern stage, especially the chorus in opera, we are totally unable to grasp how this tragic chorus could be older, more original, even more important than the real "action" (as tradition tell us so clearly), while we cannot then figure out why, given that traditionally high importance and original preeminence, that chorus would be put together only out of lowly serving creatures, at first only out of goat-like satyrs, and while for us the orchestra in front of the acting area remains a constant enigma, we have now come to the insight that the acting area together with the action is basically and originally thought of only as a vision, that the single "reality" is the chorus itself, which creates the vision out of itself and speaks of that with the entire symbolism of dance, tone, and word.

This chorus in its vision gazes at its lord and master Dionysus and is thus always the chorus of servants. The chorus sees how Dionysus, the god, suffers and glorifies himself, and thus it does not itself act. But in this role, as complete servants in relation to the god, the chorus is nevertheless the highest (that is, the Dionysian) expression of nature and, like nature, thus in its frenzy speaks the language of oracular wisdom, as the sympathetic as well as wise person reporting the truth from the heart of the world. So arises that fantastic and apparently offensive figure of the wise and frenzied satyr, who is, at the same time, "the naïve man" in contrast to the god: an image of nature and its strongest drives, a symbol of that and at the same time the announcer of its wisdom and art: musician, poet, dancer, visionary—in a single person.

According to this insight and to the tradition, Dionysus, the essential stage hero and centre of the vision, was not really present in the very oldest periods of tragedy, but was only imagined as present. That is, originally tragedy was only "chorus" and not "drama." Later the attempt was made to show the god as real and then to present in a way visible to every eye the form of the vision together with the transfiguring setting. At that point "drama" in the strict sense begins. Now the dithyrambic chorus takes on the task of stimulating the mood of the listeners right up to the Dionysian level, so that when the tragic hero appeared on the stage, they did not see something like an awkward masked person but a visionary shape born, as it were, out of their own enchantment.

If we imagine Admetus thinking deeply about his recently departed wife Alcestis and pining away in his spiritual contemplation of her, and how suddenly is led up to him an image of a woman of similar form and similar gait, but in disguise, if we imagine his sudden trembling anticipation, his emotional comparisons, his instinctive conviction—then we have an analogy to the sensation with which the aroused Dionysian spectator sees the god stride onto the stage, with whose suffering he has already become one. Spontaneously he transfers the whole picture of the god, which like magic trembles in his soul, onto that masked form and dissolves the reality of that figure as if in a ghostly unreality. This is the Apollonian dream state, in which the world of day veils itself and a new world, clearer, more comprehensible, more moving than the first, and yet shadow-like generates itself anew in a continuing series of changes before our eyes.

With this in mind, we can recognize in tragedy a drastic contrast of styles: speech, colour, movement, dynamics of speech appear in the Dionysian lyric of the chorus and also in the Apollonian dream world of the scene as expressive spheres completely separate from each other. The Apollonian illusions, in which Dionysus objectifies himself, are no longer "an eternal sea, a changing weaving motion, a glowing sense of living" (as is the case with the music of the chorus), no longer those powers which are only felt and cannot be turned into poetic images, in which the frenzied servant of Dionysus feels the approach of the god. Now, from the acting area the clarity and solemnity of the epic form speaks to him; now Dionysus no longer speaks through forces but as an epic hero, almost with the language of Homer.

9

Everything which comes to the surface in the Apollonian part of Greek tragedy, in the dialogue, looks simple, translucent, and beautiful. In this sense the dialogue is an image of the Greeks, whose nature reveals itself in dancing, because in dancing the greatest power is only latent, betraying its presence in the lithe and rich movement. The language of the Sophoclean heroes surprises us by its Apollonian clarity and brightness, so that we immediately imagine that we are glimpsing the innermost basis of their being, with some astonishment that the path to this foundation is so short.

However, once we look away from the character of the hero as it surfaces and becomes perceptible (a character which is basically nothing more than a light picture cast onto a dark wall, that is, an illusion through and through) we penetrate further into the myth which projects itself in this bright reflection. At that point we suddenly experience a phenomenon which is the reverse of a well known optical one.. When we make a determined attempt to look directly at the sun and turn away blinded, we have dark coloured specks in front of our eyes, like a remedy. Those illuminated illusory pictures of the Sophoclean heroes are the reverse of that: briefly put, the Apollonian of the mask, necessary creations of a glimpse into the inner terror of nature, are like bright spots to heal us from the horrifying night of the disabled gaze. Only in this sense can we think of correctly grasping the serious and significant idea of "Greek serenity"; whereas nowadays we run into the false idea of this as a condition of safe contentment with all of life's paths and bridges

The most painful figure of the Greek stage, the unlucky Oedipus, is understood by Sophocles as the noble man who is destined for error and misery in spite of his wisdom, but who at the end through his immense suffering exerts a beneficial effect around him which is effective on those different from him. The noble man does not sin—that's what the profound poet wishes to tell us: through Oedipus' actions every law, every natural principle of order, indeed, the entire moral world may collapse, but because of these actions a higher circle of consequences is created, which will found a new world on the ruins of the old world which has been overthrown. Insofar as the poet is also a religious thinker, that is what he says to us. As a poet, he shows us first a wonderfully complicated legal knot, which the judge, link by link, undoes, in the process destroying himself. The real joy for the Greek in this dialectical solution is so great that a sense of powerful serenity invests the entire work, which breaks the sting of the dreadful pre-conditions which started the process.

In Oedipus in Colonus we run into this same serenity, but elevated by an immeasurable transformation. Unlike the old man afflicted with excessive suffering, a man who merely suffers as the victim of everything which happens to him, now we have the unearthly serenity which descends from the sphere of the gods and indicates to us that the hero in his purely passive conduct achieves his highest action, which reaches out far over his own life (whereas his conscious striving in his earlier life led him to pure passivity). Thus for the mortal eye the inextricably tangled legal knot of the Oedipus story is slowly untangled, and the most profound human joy suffuses us with this divine dialectical companion piece..

If we have here correctly explained the poet, one can still ask whether the content of the myth has been exhausted in that explanation. And here we see that the entire conception of the poet is nothing other than that illuminated image which nature as healer holds up before us after a glimpse into the abyss. Oedipus the murderer of his father, the husband of his mother, Oedipus the solver of the riddle of the sphinx! What does the secret trinity of these fatal events tell us? There is a very ancient folk belief, especially in Persia, that a wise magus could be born only out of incest. With hindsight on Oedipus as the solver of riddles and emancipator of his mother, what we have to interpret right away is the fact that right there where, through prophecy and magical powers, the spell of present and future is broken, that rigid law of individuation and the essential magic of nature in general, then an immense natural horror (for example, incest) must have come first as the original cause. For how could we compel nature to yield up its secrets, if not for the fact that we fight back against her and win, that is, if not for the fact that we commit unnatural actions?

I see this idea stamped out in that dreadful trinity of Oedipus's three fates: the same man who solved the riddle of nature (the ambiguous sphinx) must also break the most sacred natural laws when he murders his father and marries his mother. Indeed, the myth seems to want to whisper to us that wisdom—especially Dionysian wisdom—is something horrific and hostile to nature, that a man who through his knowledge pushes nature into the destructive abyss, has to experience in himself the disintegration of nature. "The lance of knowledge turns itself against the wise man. Wisdom is a crime against nature." The myth calls out such frightening statements to us. But, like a ray of sunlight, the Greek poet touches the sublime and fearful Memnon's Column of

Myth, so that the myth suddenly begins to play out Sophoclean melodies.

Now I'm going to compare the glory of passivity with the glory of activity which illuminates Aeschylus's Prometheus.. What Aeschylus the thinker had to say to us here, but what Aeschylus as a poet could only hint at through a metaphorical picture—that's what young Goethe knew how to reveal in the bold words of his Prometheus:

"Here I sit—I make men in my own image, a race like me, to suffer, to weep, to enjoy life and rejoice, and then to pay no attention, like me."

Man, rising up into something Titanic, is victorious over his own culture and compels the gods to unite with him, because in his self-controlled wisdom he holds their existence and the limits to their authority in his hand. The most marvelous thing in that poem of Prometheus, which is, according to its basic concepts, is a hymn celebrating impiety, is, however, the deep Aeschylean impulse for justice. The immeasurable suffering of the brave "individual", on the one hand, and, on the other, the peril faced by the gods, even a presentiment of the twilight of the gods, the compelling power for a metaphysical oneness, for a reconciliation of both these worlds of suffering—all this is a powerful reminder of the central point and major claim of the Aeschylean world view, which sees fate (Moira) enthroned over gods and men as eternal justice.

With respect to the astonishing daring with which Aeschylus places the Olympian world on his scales of justice, we must remind ourselves that the deep-thinking Greek had an unshakably firm basis for metaphysical thinking in his mystery cults, and that he could unload all his skeptical moods onto the Olympians. The Greek artist, in particular, in looking back on these divinities, felt a dark sense of reciprocal dependency. And this sense is symbolized especially in Aeschylus's Prometheus. The Titanic artist (Prometheus) found in himself the defiant belief that he could make men and, at the very least, destroy Olympian gods—all this through his higher wisdom, which he, of course, was compelled to atone for in eternal suffering. The magnificent capability of the great genius, for whom eternal suffering itself is too cheap a price, the harsh pride of the artist—that is the content and soul of Aeschylean poetry; whereas, Sophocles in his

Oedipus makes his case by sounding out the victory song of the holy man.

But also this meaning which Aeschylus gave the myth does not fill the astonishing depth of its terror. The artist's joy in being, the serenity of artistic creativity in spite of that impiety, is only a light picture of cloud and sky, which mirrors itself in a dark ocean of sorrow. The Prometheus saga is a primordial possession of the Aryan population collectively and documentary evidence of their talent for the profoundly tragic. In fact, it could be the case that for the Aryan being this myth has the same defining meaning as the myth of the Fall has for the Semitic peoples, and that both myths are, to some degree, related, as brother and sister.

The pre-condition of this Prometheus myth is the extraordinary value which a naïve humanity associates with fire as the true divine protector of that rising culture. But the fact that man freely controls fire and does not receive it merely as a gift from heaven, as a stirring lightning flash or warming rays of the sun, appeared to these contemplative primitive men as an outrage, a crime against divine nature. And so right there the first philosophical problem posed an awkward insoluble contradiction between man and god and pushed it right up to the door of that culture, like a boulder. The best and loftiest thing which mankind can share is achieved through a crime, and people must now accept the further consequences, namely, the entire flood of suffering and troubles with which the offended divine presences afflict the nobly ambitious human race. Such things must happen—an austere notion which, through the value which it gives to a crime, stands in a curious contrast to the Semitic myth of the Fall, in which curiosity, lying falsehoods, temptation, lust, in short, a row of predominantly female emotions are look upon as the origin of evil.

What distinguishes the Aryan conception is the lofty view of an active transgression as the essentially Promethean virtue. With this, the ethical basis of pessimistic tragedy is established together with the justification of human evil, that is, human guilt as the penalty for that sin. The impiety in the essence of things—that's what the thinking Aryan is not inclined to quibble away. The contradiction in the heart of the world reveals itself to him as the interpenetration of different worlds, for example, a divine and human world, each one of which is right in its separate way but which must suffer for its individuality as the two worlds come close together.

With this heroic push of the individual into the universal, with this attempt to stride out over the limits of individuation and to wish to be oneself a world being, man suffers in himself the contradiction hidden in things, that is, he violates the laws and he suffers. Just as among the Aryans crime is seen as male, and among the Semites sin is seen as female, so the original crime was committed by a man, the original sin by a woman. In this connection, the chorus of witches [in Goethe's Faust] says:

We're not so particular in what we say: Woman takes a thousand steps to get her way. But no matter how quickly she hurries on, With just one leap the man will get it done.

Anyone who understands this innermost core of the Prometheus saga, namely, the imperative requirement that the individual striving like a Titan has to fall into crime, must also sense at the same time the un-Apollonian quality of this pessimistic concept. For Apollo wants to make these separate individual worlds tranquil precisely because he establishes the border line between them and, with his demands for self-knowledge and moderation, always reminds us once again of the most sacred laws of the world. However, to prevent this Apollonian tendency from freezing form into Egyptian stiffness and frigidity and to prevent the movement of the entire ocean from dying away, through the attempts of the Apollonian tendency to prescribe to the individual waves their path and extent, from time to time the high flood of the Dionysian destroys those small circles in which the one-sided Apollonian will seeks to confine the Greek spirit. Now suddenly a tidal wave of the Dionysian takes the single small individual crests on its back, just as the brother of Prometheus, the Titan Atlas, shouldered the Earth. This Titanic impulse to become something like the Atlas of all individuals and to bear them on one's wide back, higher and higher, further and further, is the common link between the Promethean and the Dionysian.

In this view, the Aeschylean Prometheus is a Dionysian mask; while, in that previously mentioned deep desire for justice Aeschylus betrays to those who understand his paternal descent from Apollo, the god of individuation and the limits of justice. And the double nature of the

Aeschylean Prometheus, his simultaneously Dionysian and Apollonian nature, can be expressed in an understandable way with the following words: "Everything present is just and unjust and both aspects are equally justified."

That is your world! That's what one calls a world!

10

It is an incontestable tradition that Greek tragedy in its oldest form had as its subject only the suffering of Dionysus and that for a long time later the individually present stage heroes were only Dionysus. But with the same certainty we can assert that right up to the time of Euripides Dionysus never ceased being the tragic hero, that all the famous figures of the Greek theatre, like Prometheus, Oedipus, and so on, are only masks of that primordial hero Dionysus. The fact that behind all these masks stands a divinity, that is the fundamental reason for the frequently admired characteristic "ideality" of those well known figures.

Someone (I don't know who) asserted that all individuals, as individuals, have to be taken as comic and thus untragic, that the Greeks in general could not tolerate individuals in their tragic theatre. In fact, they seem to have felt this way. That Platonic distinction between and evaluation of the "idea" in contrast to the "idol" in connection with likenesses lies deeply grounded in the nature of the Greeks. But for us to make use of Plato's terminology, we would have to talk of the tragic figures of the Greek stage in something like the following terms: the one truly real Dionysus appears in a multiplicity of shapes, in the mask of a struggling hero and, as it were, bound up in the nets of the individual will. So now the god made manifest talks and acts in such a way that he looks like an erring, striving, suffering individual. The fact that he appears in general with this epic definition and clarity is the effect of Apollo, the interpreter of dreams, who indicates to the chorus its Dionysian state by this metaphorical appearance.

In reality, however, that hero is the suffering Dionysus of the mysteries, that god who experiences the suffering of the individual in himself, the god about whom the amazing myths tell how he, as a child, was dismembered by the Titans and now in this condition is venerated as Zagreus. Through this is revealed the idea that this dismemberment, the essentially Dionysian suffering, is like a transformation into air, water, earth, and fire, that we also have to look upon the condition of individuation as the source and basis for all suffering, as something in itself reprehensible. From the laughing of this Dionysus arose the Olympian gods, from his tears arose mankind. In that existence as dismembered god Dionysus has the dual nature of a cruelly savage daemon and a lenient, gentle master.

The initiates in the Eleusinian mysteries hoped for a rebirth of Dionysus, which we now can understand as the mysterious end of individuation. The initiate's song of jubilation cried out to this approaching third Dionysus. And only with this hope was there a ray of joy on the face of the fragmented world, torn apart into individuals, just as myth reveals in the picture of the eternal sorrow of sunken Demeter, who rejoices again for the first time when someone says to her that she might be able once again to give birth to Dionysus. In these established concepts we already have assembled all the components of a profound and pessimistic world view, together with the mysterious teachings of tragedy: the basic acknowledgement of the unity of all existing things, the idea of individuation as the ultimate foundation of all evil, art as the joyful hope that the spell of individuation is there for us to break, as a premonition of a re-established unity.

It has been pointed out earlier that the Homeric epic is the poetry of Olympian culture, with which it sang its own song of victory over the terrors of the fight against the Titans. Now, under the overwhelming influence of tragic poetry, the Homeric myths were newly reborn and show in this metamorphosis that by now the Olympian culture is overcome by an even deeper world view. The defiant Titan Prometheus reported to his Olympian torturer that for the first time his rule was threatened by the highest danger, unless he quickly joined forces with him. In Aeschylus we acknowledge the union of the frightened Zeus, worried about the end of his power, with the Titan.

Thus the earlier age of the Titans is belatedly brought back from Tartarus into the light once more. The philosophy of wild and naked nature looks with the unconcealed countenance of truth at the myths of the Homeric world dancing past it. Before the flashing eyes of this goddess, those myths grow pale and tremble, until they press the mighty fist of the Dionysian artist into the service of the new divinity. The Dionysian truth takes over the entire realm of myth as the symbol of its knowledge and speaks of this knowledge, partly in the public culture of the tragedy and partly in the secret celebrations of the dramatic mystery celebrations, but always in the disguise of the old myths. What power was it which liberated Prometheus from his vultures and transformed myth to a vehicle of Dionysian wisdom? It was the Herculean power of music. Music, which attained its highest manifestation in tragedy, had the power to interpret myth with a new significance in the most profound manner, something we have already described before as the most powerful capacity of music.

For it is the lot of every myth gradually to creep into the crevice of an assumed historical reality and to become analyzed as a unique fact in answer to the historical demands of some later time or other. The Greek were already fully on their way to labeling cleverly and arbitrarily the completely mythical dreams of their youth as historical, pragmatic, and youthful history. For this is the way religions tend to die out, namely, when the mythical pre-conditions of a religion, under the strong, rational eyes of an orthodox dogmatism become classified as a closed totality of historical events and people begin anxiously to defend the credibility of their myths, but to resist the naturally continuing life and growth of those myths, and when the feeling for the myth dies out and in its place the claim to put religion on a historical footing steps onto the scene.

The newly born genius of Dionysian music now seized these dying myths, and in its hands myth blossomed again, with colours which it had never shown before, with a scent which stirred up a longing premonition of a metaphysical world. After this last flourishing, myth collapsed, its leaves grew pale, and soon the mocking Lucians of antiquity grabbed up the flowers, scattered around by all winds, colourless and withered. Through tragedy myth attains its most profound content, its most expressive form. It lifts itself up again, like a wounded hero, and with the excessive power and wise tranquilly of a dying man, its eyes burn with its last powerful light.

What did you want, you rascal Euripides, when you sought to force this dying man once more into your service? He died under your powerful hands. And now you had to use a counterfeit, masked myth, which was able only to dress itself up with the old splendour, like Hercules's monkey. And as myth died with you, so died the genius of music as well. Even though you plundered with greedy hands all the gardens of music, you achieved only a counterfeit masked music. And because you abandoned Dionysus, you were then abandoned by Apollo. Even if you hunted out all the passions from their beds and charmed them into your circle, even though you sharpened and filed a really sophisticated dialectic for the speeches of your heroes, nevertheless your heroes have only counterfeit, masked passions and speak only a counterfeit, masked language.

11

Greek tragedy died in a manner different from all its ancient sister arts: it died by suicide, as a result of an insoluble (hence tragic) conflict; whereas, all the others passed away in advanced old age with the most beautiful and tranquil deaths. If it is an appropriately happy natural condition to depart from life with beautiful descendants and without any painful strains in one's life, the end of those ancient artistic genres manifests to us such a fortunate natural state of things. They disappeared slowly, and their more beautiful children were already standing there before their dying gaze, impatiently lifting their heads in courageous gestures. By contrast, with the death of Greek tragedy there was created an immense emptiness, profoundly felt everywhere. Just as the Greek sailors at the time of Tiberius heard from some isolated island the shattering cry "The great god Pan is dead," so now, like a painful lament, rang out throughout the Greek world, "Tragedy is dead! Poetry itself is lost with it! Away, away with you, you stunted, emaciated epigones! Off with you to hell, so you can for once eat your fill of the crumbs from your former masters!"

If now a new form of art blossomed which paid tribute to tragedy as its predecessor and mistress, it was looked upon with fright, because while it carried the characteristics of its mother, they were the same ones she had shown in her long death struggle. Tragedy's death struggle was fought by Euripides, and this later art form is known as New Attic Comedy. In it the atrophied form of tragedy lived on, as a monument to tragedy's extremely laborious and violent death.

Looking at things this way makes understandable the passionate fondness the poets of the newer comedies felt for Euripides. Thus, Philemon's wish (to be hanged immediately so that he could seek out Euripides in the underworld, provided only he could be convinced that the dead man was still in possession of his wits) is no longer something strange. However, if we ask ourselves to indicate, briefly and without claiming to say anything in detail, what Euripides might have in common with Menander and Philemon and what was so excitingly exemplary and effective for them in Euripides, it is enough to say that the spectator in Euripides is brought up onto the stage. Anyone who recognizes the material out of which the Promethean tragedians before Euripides created their heroes and how remote from them was any intention of bringing the true mask of reality onto the stage will see clearly the totally deviant tendencies of Euripides.

As a result of Euripides, the man of ordinary life pushed his way out of the spectators' space and up onto the acting area. The mirror in which earlier only great and bold features had been shown now displayed a painful fidelity which conscientiously reflected the unsuccessful features of nature. Odysseus, the typical Greek of the older art, now sank in the hands of the newer poets into the figure of Graeculus, who from now on stands right at the centre of dramatic interest as the good hearted, clever slave. What Euripides in Aristophanes' Frogs gives himself credit for as a service, namely, that through his household medicines he freed tragic art of its pompous hustle and bustle, that point we can trace above all in his tragic heroes.

Essentially the spectator now saw and heard his double on the Euripidean stage and was happy that that character understood how to talk so well. But this was not the only delight. People themselves learned from Euripides how to speak. He praises himself on this very point in the contest with Aeschylus—how through him the people learned to observe in an artistic way, with the keenest sophistication, to judge, and to draw consequences. Because of this complete transformation in public language he also made the new comedy possible. For from that time on there was nothing mysterious about how ordinary life could appear on stage and what language it would use.

Middle-class mediocrity, on which Euripides built all his political hopes, now came into prominence. Up to that point, in tragedy the demi-god and in comedy the intoxicated satyr or semi-human had determined the nature of the language. And so the Aristophanic Euripides gave himself high praise for how he presented common, well-known, ordinary living and striving, which any person was capable of judging. If now the entire crowd philosophized, administered their lands and goods with tremendous astuteness, and carried on their own legal matters, well then, he claimed, that was to his credit and the achievement of the wisdom which he had drummed into the people.

The new comedy could now direct its attention to such a prepared and enlightened crowd, for whom Euripides became, to some extent, the choir master. Only this time the chorus of spectators had to have practice. As soon as the chorus was well trained to sing in the Euripidean musical key, a style of drama like a chess game arose, the new comedy, with its continuing triumph of sly shrewdness. But Euripides, the leader of the chorus, was incessantly praised. Indeed, people would have let themselves be killed in order to learn more from him, if they had not been aware that tragic poets were just as dead as tragedy itself.

With tragedy the Greeks had surrendered their faith in immortality, not merely the faith in an ideal past, but also the faith in an ideal future. The saying from the well-known written epitaph, "as an old man negligent and trivial" is applicable also to the old age of Hellenism. The instantaneous, the witty, the foolish, and the capricious—these are its loftiest divinities, the fifth state, that of the slave (or at least the feelings of a slave) now come to rule. And if it is possible to talk still of a "Greek serenity," it is the serenity of the slave, who has no idea how to take responsibility for anything difficult, how to strive for anything great, or how to value anything in the past or future higher than the present.

It was this appearance of "Greek serenity" which so outraged the profound and fearful natures of the first four centuries of Christianity. To them this feminine flight from seriousness and terror, this cowardly self-satisfaction with comfortable consumption, seemed not only despicable but also the essentially anti-Christian frame of mind. And to the influence of this outrage we can ascribe the fact that the view of

Greek antiquity as a time of rose-coloured serenity lasted for centuries with almost invincible tenacity, as if Greek antiquity had never produced a sixth century, with its birth of tragedy, its mystery cults, its Pythagoras and Heraclitus, indeed, as if the artistic works of the great age simply did not exist—although these works, each and every one of them, cannot be explained at all on the grounds of such a senile joy in existence and serenity, moods appropriate to a slave, or of things which testify to a completely different world view as the basis of their existence.

Finally, when it is asserted that Euripides brought the spectator onto the stage in order to make him really capable for the first time of judging drama, it may appear as if the older tragic art had not resolved its false relationship to the spectator, and people might be tempted to value the radical tendency of Euripides to attain an appropriate relationship between the art work and the public as a progressive step beyond Sophocles. However, the "public" is only a word and not at all a constant, firm thing of value. Why should an artist be duty-bound to accommodate himself to a power whose strength is only in numbers? And if, with respect to his talent and intentions, he senses that he is superior to every one of these spectators, how could he feel more respect for the common expression of all these capacities inferior to his own than for the most highly talented individual spectator. To tell the truth, no Greek artist handled his public over a long lifetime with greater daring and self-satisfaction than Euripides. As the masses threw themselves at his feet, he nonetheless, with a sublime act of defiance, threw his own individual attitudes in their faces, those same attitudes with which he had conquered the masses. If this genius had had the slightest reverence for the pandemonium of the public, he would have broken apart under the cudgel blows of his failures long before the middle of his lifetime.

Taking this into account, we see that our expression—Euripides brought the spectator onto the stage, in order to make the spectator capable of making judgments—was only provisional and that we have to seek out a deeper understanding of his dramatic tendencies. By contrast, it is well known everywhere how Aeschylus and Sophocles during their lifetime and, indeed, well beyond that, stood in full possession of popular favour, and thus, given these predecessors of

Euripides, there is no point in talking about a misunderstanding between the art work and the public. What drove the richly talented artist (Euripides), constantly under the urge to create, away from the path above which shone the sun of the greatest poetic names and the cloudless sky of popular approval? What curious consideration of the spectator led him to go against the spectator? How could he be contemptuous of his public out of a high respect for his public?

The solution to the riddle posed immediately above is this: Euripides felt himself as a poet higher than the masses, but not higher than two of his spectators. He brought the masses up onto the stage. Those two spectators he honoured as the only judges capable of rendering a verdict and as the masters of all his art. Following their instructions and reminders, he transposed the entire world of feelings, passions, and experiences, which up to that point had appeared in the rows of spectators as an invisible chorus in every celebratory presentation, into the souls of his stage heroes. Following the demands of these two judges, he sought out for his heroes new characters, a new language, and a new tone. In the vote of these two spectators alone he heard judgment pronounced on his creation, just as much as he heard encouragement promising victory, when he saw himself once again condemned by the justice of the general public.

The first of these two spectators is Euripides himself, Euripides the thinker, not the poet. Of him we can say that the extraordinarily richness of his critical talent, like that of Lessing, constantly stimulated, even if it did not create, an additional productive artistic drive. With this talent, with all the clarity and agility of his critical thinking, Euripides sat in the theatre and struggled to recognize the masterpieces of his great predecessors, as with a painting darkened by age, feature by feature, line by line. And here he encountered something familiar to those who know the profound secrets of Aeschylean tragedy: he became aware of something incommensurable in each feature and in each line, a certain deceptive clarity and, at the same time, an enigmatic depth, the infinity of the background.

The clearest figure still always had a comet's tail attached to it, which seemed to hint at the unknown, the inexplicable. The same duality lay over the construction of the drama, as well as over the meaning of the chorus. And how ambiguously the solution of the ethical problems remained for him. How questionable the handling of the myths! How unequal the division of luck and disaster! Even in the language of the old tragedies there was a great deal he found offensive or, at least, enigmatic. He especially found too much pomp and circumstance for simple relationships, too many figures of speech and monstrosities for the straightforward characters. So he sat there in the theatre, full of uneasy thoughts, and, as a spectator, he came to realize that he did not understand his great predecessors. Since his reason counted for him as the root of all enjoyment and creativity, he had to ask himself and look around to see if there was anyone who thought the way he did and could in the same way attest to that incommensurability of the old drama.

But the public, including the best individuals among them, met him only with a suspicious smile. No one could explain to him why his reflections about and objections to the great masters might be correct. And in this agonizing condition he found the other spectator, who did not understand tragedy and therefore did not value it. United with him, Euripides could dare to begin emerging from his isolation to fight the immense battle against the art works of Aeschylus and Sophocles—not with critical writings, but as a dramatic poet, who sets up the presentation of his tragedy in opposition to the tradition.

12

Before we designate this other spectator by name, let's linger here a moment to reconsider that characteristic duality and incommensurability at the heart of Aeschylean tragedy (something we described earlier). Let us think about how strange we find the chorus and the hero of those tragedies, which were not able to reconcile with what we are used to or with our traditions, until we recognized that duality itself as the origin and essence of Greek tragedy, as the expression of two artistic drives woven together, the Apollonian and the Dionysian.

To cut that primordial and all-powerful Dionysian element out of tragedy and to rebuild tragedy as a pure, new, and un-Dionysian art, morality, and world view—that has now revealed itself to us very clearly as the tendency of Euripides. Near the end of his life, Euripides himself propounded as emphatically as possible the question about the value and meaning of this tendency in a myth to his contemporaries. Should the Dionysian exist at all? Should we not eradicate it forcefully from Greek soil? Of course we should, the poet says to us, if only it were possible, but the god Dionysus is too powerful. The most intelligent opponent, like Pentheus in the Bacchae, is unexpectedly charmed by Dionysus and runs from him in this enchanted state to his destruction.

The judgment of the two old men, Cadmus and Tiresias, seems also to be the judgment of the aged poet: the mind of the cleverest individual does not throw away that old folk tradition, that eternally propagating reverence for Dionysus; indeed, where such amazing powers are concerned, it is appropriate at least to demonstrate a diplomatically prudent show of joining in. But even with that, the god might still possibly take offense at such a lukewarm participation and transform the diplomat finally into a dragon (as happens here with Cadmus).

The poet tells us this, a poet who fought throughout his long life against Dionysus with heroic force, only to conclude his life finally with a glorification of his opponent and a suicide, like a man suffering from vertigo who, in order to escape the dreadful dizziness, which he can no longer endure, throws himself off a tower. That tragedy is a protest against the practicality of his artistic program, and that program had already succeeded! A miracle had taken place: just when the poet recanted, his program was already victorious. Dionysus had already been chased off the tragic stage, and by a daemonic power speaking out from Euripides. But Euripides was, to some extent, only a mask. The divinity which spoke out of him was not Dionysus, and not Apollo, but an entirely new-born daemon called Socrates.

This is the new opposition: the Dionysian and the Socratic. And from this contrast, Greek tragedy perished as a work of art. No matter now how much Euripides might seek to console us with his retraction, he was unsuccessful. The most magnificent temple lay in ruins. What use to us are the laments of the destroyer and his awareness that it had been the most beautiful of all temples? And even if Euripides himself, as a punishment, has been turned into a dragon by the artistic critics of all ages, who can be satisfied with this paltry compensation?

Let's get closer now to this Socratic project, with which Euripides fought against and conquered Aeschylean tragedy.

What purpose (that's the question we need to ask at this point) could Euripides' intention to ground drama solely on the un-Dionysian have had, if we assume its implementation had the very highest ideals? What form of drama remained, if it was not to be born from the womb of music, in that mysterious half-light of the Dionysian? All it could be was dramatic epic, an Apollonian art form in which the tragical effect is naturally unattainable.

This is not a matter of the content of the represented events. I might even assert that in Goethe's proposed Nausikaa it would have been impossible to make the suicide of that idyllic being (which was to be carried out in the fifth act) grippingly tragic, for the power of the Apollonian epic is so extraordinary that it magically transforms the most horrific things through that joy in and redemption through appearances right before our very eyes. The poet of the dramatic epic cannot completely fuse with his pictures, any more than the epic rhapsodist can. It is always a matter of still calm, tranquil contemplation with open eyes, a state which sees the images in front of it. The actor in this dramatic epic remains, in the most profound sense, still a rhapsodist; the consecration of the inner dream lies upon all his actions, so that he is never completely an actor.

How is Euripides' work related with respect to this ideal of Apollonian drama? It is just like the relationship of the solemn rhapsodist of the olden times to the younger attitude, whose nature is described in Plato's Ion: "When I say something sad, my eyes fill with tears. But if what I say is horrifying and terrible, then the hairs on my head stand on end from fright, and my heart knocks." Here we do not see any more the epic dissolution of the self in appearances, the disinterested coolness of the real actor, who remain, even in his highest achievements, totally appearance and delight in appearances. Euripides is the actor with the beating heart, with his hair standing on end. He designs his work as a Socratic thinker, and he carries it out as a passionate actor.

Euripides is a pure artist neither in planning his work nor in carrying it out. Thus the Euripidean drama is simultaneously a cool and fiery thing, equally capable of freezing or burning. It is impossible for it to attain the Apollonian effect of the epic, while, on the other hand, it has divorced itself as much as possible from the Dionysian elements, and now, in order to work at all, it needs new ways to arouse people, methods which can no longer lie within either of the two individual artistic drives of the Apollonian and the Dionysian. These method of arousing people are detached paradoxical ideas, substituted for Apollonian objects of contemplation, and fiery emotional effects, substituted for Dionysian enchantment. The fiery effects are, to be sure, imitated with a high degree of realism, but the ideas and emotional effects are not in the slightest way imbued with the spirit of art.

If we have now recognized that Euripides did not succeed in basing his drama solely on Apollonian principles, that his un-Dionysian tendencies much rather led him astray into an inartistic naturalism, we are now able to move closer to the essential quality of his Socratic aesthetics, whose most important law runs something like this: "Everything must be understandable in order to be beautiful," a corollary to the Socratic saying, "Only the knowledgeable person is virtuous." With this canon at hand, Euripides measured all the individual features and justified them according to this principle: the language, characters, dramatic construction, the choral music.

What we habitually assess so frequently in Euripides, in comparison with Sophoclean tragedy, as a poetical deficiency and a backward step is for the most part the product of his emphatic critical process, his daring intelligence. Let the Euripi dean prologue serve as an example of what that rationalistic method produces. Nothing can be more offensive to our stage techniques than the prologue in Euripides's plays. That a single person should step forward at the beginning of a work and explain who he is, what has gone on before the action starts, what has happened up to this point, and even what will occur in the unfolding of the work, that would strike a modern poetical dramatist as a wanton, inexcusable abandonment of all the effects of suspense. If we know everything which is going to happen, who will want to sit around waiting to see that it really does happen? For here there is nothing like the stimulating relationship between a prophetic dream and a later real event. Euripides thought quite differently about the matter.

The effect of tragedy never depends on epic suspense, on the tempting uncertainty about what will happen now and later. It depends far more on those great rhetorical-lyrical scenes in which the passion and dialectic of the main hero swelled up into a wide and powerful storm. Everything was preparing for pathos, not for action. What did not prepare the way for paths was considered disposable. But what hinders most seriously the listener's delighted devotion to such scenes is any missing part, any gap in the network of the previous events. As long as the listener still has to figure out what this or that person means, what gives rise to this or that conflict in motives or purposes, then his full immersion in the suffering and action of the main character, his breathless sympathy with and fear for them are not possible. The Aeschylean-Sophoclean tragedies made use of the most elegant artistic methods in the opening scenes to provide the spectators, as if by chance, all the necessary clues to understand everything, a technique in which their noble artistry proves its worth by allowing the necessary features to appear, but, so to speak, as something masked and accidental.

But Euripides still believed he noticed that during these first scenes the spectator was oddly disturbed having to figure out the simple arithmetic of the previous events so that the poetical beauties and the pathos of the exposition was lost on him. Therefore Euripides set up the prologue even before the exposition and put it in the mouth of a person whom people could trust—a divinity would necessarily confirm the outcome of the tragedy for the public, more or less, and take away any doubts about the reality of the myth, in a manner similar to the way in which Descartes could establish the reality of the empirical world through an appeal to the truthfulness of God and his inability to lie. At the end of his drama, Euripides once again made use of this same divine truthfulness in order to confirm his hero's future for the public. That is the task of the notorious deus ex machina. Between the epic prologue and epilogue lay the lyrical, dramatic present, the essential "drama."

So Euripides as a poet is, above all, the echo of his conscious knowledge, and it is precisely this which confers upon him such a memorable place in the history of Greek art.

In view of his critically productive creativity it must have often struck him that he must be bringing alive in drama the opening of Anaxagoras's text, the first lines of which go as follows: "In the beginning everything was a confused mixture, but then came reason and created order." And if, among philosophers, Anaxagoras, with his concept of mind, seems to be the first sober man among total drunkards, so Euripides might have conceptualized his relationship to the other poets with a similar image. So long as the single creator of order and ruler of all, the mind, was still excluded from artistic creativity, everything was still mixed up in a chaotic primordial pudding. That's how Euripides must have thought about it; that's how he, the first "sober" poet must have passed sentence on the "drunken" poets.

What Sophocles said about Aeschylus—that he does what's right, without being aware of it—was certainly not said in any Euripidean sense. Euripides would have conceded only that Aeschylus created improperly because he created without any conscious awareness. Even the god-like Plato speaks of the creative capability of poets and how this is not a conscious understanding, but for the most part only ironically, and he draws a comparison with the talent of prophets and dream interpreters, for the poet is not able to write until he has lost his conscious mind and reason no longer resides in him. Euripides undertook the task (which Plato also took on) to show the world the opposite of the "irrational" poet. His basic aesthetic principle, "everything must be conscious in order to be beautiful," is, as I have said, the corollary to the Socratic saying, "Everything must be conscious in order to be good."

With this in mind, it is permissible for us to assess Euripides as the poet of Socratic aesthetics. Socrates, however, was that second spectator, who did not understand the old tragedy and therefore did not value it. With Socrates as his ally, Euripides dared to be the herald of a new artistic creativity. If old tragedy perished in this development, then Socratic aesthetics is the murdering principle. Insofar as the fight was directed against the Dionysian of the older art, we recognize in Socrates the enemy of Dionysus, the new Orpheus, who roused himself against Dionysus, and who, although destined to be torn apart by the maenads of the Athenian Court of Justice, nevertheless himself made the powerful god fly away. Dionysus, as before, when he fled from Lycurgus, King of the Edoni, saved himself in the depths of the sea, that is, in the mysterious floods of a secret cult which would gradually overrun the entire world.

13

That Socrates had a close relationship to Euripides' project did not escape their contemporaries in ancient times, and the clearest expression for this happy intuition is the rumour floating around Athens that Socrates was in the habit of helping Euripides with his poetry. Both names were invoked by the supporters of the "good old days" when it was time to list the present popular leaders whose influence had brought about a situation in which the old strength of mind and body manifested at the Battle of Marathon was being increasingly sacrificed for a dubious way of explaining things, in a continuing erosion of the physical and mental powers.

This was the tone—half indignation, half contempt—in which Aristophanic comedy habitually talked of these men, to the irritation of the newer generations, who, although happy enough to betray Euripides, were always totally amazed that Socrates appeared in Aristophanes as the first and most important sophist, the mirror and essence of all sophistic ambitions. As a result, they took consolation in putting Aristophanes himself in the stocks as an impudent lying Alcibiades of poetry. Without here defending the profound instinct of Aristophanes against such attacks, I will proceed to demonstrate the close interrelationship between Socrates and Euripides as the ancients saw it.. It's particularly important to remember in this connection that Socrates, as an opponent of tragic art, never attended the performance of a tragedy, and only joined the spectators when a new piece by Euripides was being produced. The best known connection, however, is the close juxtaposition of both names in the oracular pronouncements of the Delphic Oracle, which indicated that Socrates was the wisest of men and at the same time delivered the judgment that Euripides captured second prize in the contest for wisdom.

Sophocles was the third person named in this hierarchy, the man who could praise himself in comparison with Aeschylus by saying that he (Sophocles) did what was right because he knew what was right.

Obviously the degree of clarity in these men's knowledge was the factor that designated them collectively as the three "wise men" of their time.

But the most pointed statement about this new and unheard of high opinion of knowledge and reason was uttered by Socrates, when he claimed that he was the only person to assert that he knew nothing; whereas, in his critical wandering about in Athens conversing with the greatest statesmen, orators, poets, and artists, everywhere he ran into people who imagined they knew things. Astonished, he recognized that all these famous people had no correct and clear insight into their occupations and carried out their work instinctually. "Only from instinct"— with this expression we touch upon the heart and centre of the Socratic project.

With this expression Socratic thought condemns existing art as well as contemporary ethics. Wherever he directs his searching gaze, he sees a lack of insight and the power of delusion, and from this he infers the inner falsity and worthlessness of present conditions. On the basis of this one point, Socrates believed he had to correct existence. He, one solitary individual, stepped forward with an expression of contempt and superiority, as the pioneer of a brand new style of culture, art, and morality, into that world, a scrap of which we would count it an honour to catch.

That is the immensely disturbing thing which grips us about Socrates whenever we run into him and which over and over again always stimulates us to find out the meaning and intention of this man, the most problematic figure of ancient times. Who is the man who can dare, as an individual, to deny the very essence of Greece, which with Homer, Pindar, Aeschylus, Phidias, Pericles, Pythia, and Dionysus is certainly worthy of our highest veneration? What daemonic force is it that could dare to sprinkle this magic drink into the dust? What demi-god is it to whom the ghostly chorus of the noblest specimens of humanity had to cry out: "Alas, alas! You have destroyed our beautiful world with your mighty fist. It is collapsing, falling to pieces!"

A key to the heart of Socrates is offered by that amazing phenomenon indicated by the term Socrates's daimonon. Under special circumstances in which his immense reasoning power was stalled in doubt, he resolved his irresolution firmly with a divine voice which expressed itself at such times. When this voice came, it always sounded a cautionary note. In this totally strange character instinctive wisdom reveals itself only in order to confront the conscious knowledge now and then as an impediment. Whereas in all productive men instinct is the truly creative and affirming power, and consciousness acts as a critical and cautioning reaction, in Socrates the instinct becomes the critic, consciousness becomes the creator—truly a monstrous defect.

Now, we see here a grotesque defect in mythical consciousness, so that Socrates can be considered specifically a non-mystic man in whom the logical character has become too massive through excessive use, just like instinctive wisdom in the mystic. On the other hand, it was impossible for that logical drive, as it appeared in Socrates, to turn against itself. In its unfettered rush it demonstrates a natural power of the sort we meet, to our shuddering surprise, only in the very greatest instinctive powers. Anyone who has sensed in the Platonic texts the merest scent of the god-like naïveté and confidence in the direction of Socrates's teaching has also felt how that immense drive wheel of Socratic logic is, at it were, in motion behind Socrates and how we have to see this behind Socrates, as if we were looking through a shadow.

That he himself had a premonition of this relationship comes out in the dignified seriousness with which he assessed his divine calling everywhere, even before his judges. To censure him for this is as impossible as it is to approve of his influence on the removal of instinct. When Socrates was hauled before the assembly of the Greek state, there was only one form of sentence for this irreconcilable conflict, namely, banishment. People should have expelled him beyond the borders as something enigmatic, unclassifiable, and inexplicable, so that some future world could not justly charge the Athenians with acting shamefully.

The fact that death and not exile was pronounced over him Socrates himself appears to have brought about, fully clear about what he was doing and without the natural horror of death. He went to his death with the same tranquility Plato describes him showing as he leaves the Symposium, the last drinker in the early light of dawn, beginning a new day, while behind him, on the benches and the ground, his sleeping dinner companions stay behind, to dream of Socrates the truly erotic man. The dying Socrates was the new ideal of the noble Greek youth, never seen before. Right in the vanguard, the typical Greek youth, Plato, prostrated himself before Socrates's picture with all the fervent adoration of his passionately enthusiastic soul.

14

Let's now imagine that one great Cyclops eye of Socrates focused on tragedy, that eye in which the beautiful madness of artistic enthusiasm never glowed—let's imagine how it was impossible for that eye to peer into the Dionysian abyss with a feeling of pleasure. Then what must that eye have seen in the "lofty and highly praised" tragic art, as Plato calls it? Something really unreasonable, with causes without effects, actions which apparently had no causes, and as a whole so varied and with so many different elements that any reasonable person had to reject it, but dangerous tinder for sensitive and easily excitable minds. We know which single form of poetry Socrates understood: Aesop's fables. And no doubt his reaction involved that smiling complacency with which the noble and good Gellert in his fable of the bee and the hen sings the praises of poetry:

You see in me the use of poetry— To tell the man without much sense A picture image of the truth of things.

But for Socrates tragic art did not seem "to speak the truth" at all, apart from the fact that it did address itself to those "without much sense," and thus not to philosophers, a double excuse to keep one's distance from it. Like Plato, he assigned it to the art of cosmetics, which present only a pleasant surface, not the useful, and he therefore demanded that his disciples abstain and stay away from such unphilosophical temptations, with so much success that the young poet of tragedy, Plato, immediately burned his poetical writing in order to be able to become Socrates's student. But where invincible talents fought against the Socratic instructions, his power, together with the force of his immense personality, was always still strong enough to force poetry itself into new attitudes, unknown up until then.

An example of this is Plato himself. To be sure, in his condemnation of tragedy and art in general he did not remain back behind the naïve cynicism of his master. But completely from artistic necessity he had to create an art form related directly to the existing art forms which he had rejected. The major criticism which Plato made about the old art—that it was the imitation of an illusion and thus belonged to a lower level than the empirical world—must above all not be directed against his new work of art. And so we see Plato exerting himself to go beyond reality and to present the Idea which forms basis of that pseudo-reality.

With that, however, the thinker Plato reached by a detour the very place where, as a poet, he had always been at home and from where Sophocles and all the old art was protesting against Plato's criticism. If tragedy had assimilated all earlier forms of art, so the same holds true, in an odd way, for Plato's dialogues, which were created from a mixture of all available styles and forms and hover between explanation, lyric, drama, prose and poetry, right in the middle, and in so doing broke through the strict old law about the unity of stylistic form. The Cynic philosophers went even further along the same path. With their excessively garish and motley collection of styles, weaving back and forth between prose and metrical forms, they produced the literary image of "raving Socrates," which they were in the habit of presenting in their own lives.

The Platonic dialogue was, so to speak, the boat on which the shipwreck of the old poetry, along with all its children, was saved. Pushed together into a single narrow space and with an anxious Socrates at the helm they humbly set off now into a new world, which never could see enough fantastic images of this event. Plato really gave all later worlds the image of a new form of art, the image of the novel, which can be characterized as an infinitely intensified Aesopian fable, in which the relative priorities of poetry and dialectical philosophy were the same as the relative priorities of that very philosophy and theology for many hundreds of years. Poetry, in other words, was subservient. This was poetry's new position, the place into which Plato forced it under the influence of the daemonic Socrates.

Now philosophical ideas grew up around art and forced it to cling to the trunk of dialectic. Apollonian tendencies metamorphosed into logical systematizing, something corresponding to what we noticed with Euripides, as well as a translation of the Dionysian into naturalistic effects. Socrates, the dialectical hero in Platonic drama, reminds us of the changed nature of the Euripidean hero, who has to defend his actions with reasons and counter-reasons and thus frequently runs the risk of losing our tragic sympathy. For who can fail to recognize the optimistic element in the heart of dialectic, which celebrates a jubilee with every conclusion and can breathe only in a cool conscious brightness, that optimistic element, which, once pushed into tragedy, gradually overruns its Dionysian regions and necessarily drives them to self-destruction, right to their death leap into middle-class drama.

Let people merely recall the consequences of the Socratic sayings "Virtue is knowledge; sin arises only from ignorance; the virtuous person is the happy person." In these three basic forms of optimism lies the death of tragedy. For now the virtuous hero must be a dialectician. Now there must be a perceptible link between virtue and knowledge, belief and morality. Now the transcendental vision of justice in Aeschylus is lowered to the flat and impertinent principle of "poetical justice" with its customary deus ex machina.

What does this new Socratic optimistic stage world look like with respect to the chorus and the whole musical-Dionysian basis for tragedy in general? All that seem to be something accidental, a reminder of the origin of tragedy which we can well do without, because we have come to realize that the chorus can be understood only as the origin of tragedy and the tragic in general. Already in Sophocles the chorus reveals itself as something of an embarrassment, an important indication that even with him the Dionysian stage of tragedy was beginning to fall apart. He did not dare to trust the Chorus to carry the major share of the action, but limited its role to such an extent that it appears almost as one of the actors, just as if it had been lifted out of the orchestra into the scene. This feature naturally destroys its nature completely, no matter how much Aristotle approved of this arrangement of the chorus.

This demotion in the position of the chorus, which Sophocles certainly recommended in his dramatic practice and, according to tradition, even in a written text, is the first step toward the destruction of the chorus, whose phases in Euripides, Agathon, and the New Comedy followed with breakneck speed one after the other. Optimistic dialectic, with its syllogistic whip, drove music out of tragedy, that is, it destroyed the essence of tragedy, which can be interpreted only as a manifestation and imaginary presentation of Dionysian states, as a perceptible symbolizing of music, as the dream world of a Dionysian intoxication.

We have noticed an anti-Dionysian tendency already effective before Socrates, which only achieves in him an expression of incredible brilliance. Now we must not shrink back from the question of where such a phenomenon as Socrates points. For we are not in a position, given the Platonic dialogues, to see that phenomenon as a force of totally negative dissolution. And so, while it's true that the immediate effect of the Socratic drive was to bring about the destruction of Dionysian tragedy, the profound living experiences of Socrates himself force us to the question whether or not there must necessarily be only an antithetical relationship between Socrates's doctrines and art and whether the birth of an "artistic Socrates" is in general something of a contradiction.

Where culture is concerned, that despotic logician now and then had the feeling of a gap, an emptiness, a partial sense of reproach for a duty he might have neglected. As he explains to his friends in prison, often one and the same dream apparition came to him, always with the words, "Socrates, practise music!" He calmed himself, right up to his last days, with the interpretation that his philosophizing was the highest musical art, and believed that it was incorrect that a divinity would remind him of "common, popular music." Finally in prison he came to understand how, in order to relieve his conscience completely, to practice that music which he had considered insignificant. And in this mood, he composed a poem to Apollo and rendered a few of Aesop's fables in verse.

What drove him to this practice was something like the voice of his warning daemon. It was his Apollonian insight that, like a barbarian king, he did not understand a divine image and was in danger of sinning against a divinity through his failure to understand. That statement of Socrates's dream vision is the single indication of his thinking about something perhaps beyond the borders of his logical nature. So he had to ask himself: Have I always labeled unintelligible things I could not understand? Perhaps there is a kingdom of wisdom which is forbidden to the logician? Perhaps art is even a necessary correlative and supplement to scientific understanding?

15

In the sense of this last ominous question we must how discuss how the influence of Socrates has spread out over later worlds, right up to the present and even into all future ages, like a constantly growing shadow in the evening sun, and how that influence always makes necessary the re-creation of art (I mean art in its most profound and widest metaphysical sense) and through its own immortality guarantees the immortality of art. For this fact to be acknowledged, before it was established that all art inherently depended on the Greeks, from Homer right up to Socrates, we had to deal with these Greeks as the Athenians dealt with Socrates. Almost every age and cultural stage has at some time or another sought in an ill-tempered frame of mind to free itself of the Greeks, because in comparison with the Greeks, all their achievements, apparently fully original and admired in all sincerity, suddenly appeared to lose their colour and life and were reduced to unsuccessful copies, even caricatures.

And so a heartfelt inner anger constantly kept breaking out against that arrogant little nation which dared throughout time to define everything that was not produced in its own country as "barbaric" Who were these Greeks, people asked themselves, who had achieved only an ephemeral historical glitter, only ridiculously restricted institutions, only an ambiguous competence in morality, who could even be identified with hateful vices, yet who had nevertheless taken a pre-eminent place among nations for their value and special importance, something fitted for a genius among the masses? Unfortunately people were not lucky enough to find the cup of hemlock which can do away with such a being, for all the poisons they created—envy, slander, and inner anger—were insufficient to destroy that self-satisfied magnificence.

Hence, confronted by the Greeks, people have been ashamed and afraid. It seems that an individual who values the truth above everything else might dare to propose as true the notion that the Greeks drive the chariot of our culture and every other one, but that almost always the wagon and the horses are inferior material and cannot match the glory of their drivers, who then consider it funny to whip such a team into the abyss, over which they themselves jump with a leap worthy of Achilles.

To demonstrate that Socrates also merits such a place among the drivers of the chariot, it is sufficient to recognize him as typifying a form of existence inconceivable before him, the type known as Theoretical Man. Our next task is to reach some insight about the meaning and purpose of such a man. The theoretical man, like the artist, takes an infinite satisfaction in the present and is, like the artist, protected by that satisfaction from the practical effects of pessimism with its lynx eyes which glow only in the darkness. But while the artist, in his revelation of the truth, always keeps his enchanted gaze hanging on what still remains hidden after his revelation, theoretical man enjoys and remains satisfied with the covers which have been thrown off and takes his greatest delight in the process of continually successful unveiling, a success which his own power has brought about.

There would be no scientific knowledge if it concerned itself only with that one naked goddess and had nothing else to do. For then its disciples would have to feel like those people who want to dig a hole straight through the earth, and one among them sees that, even with the greatest lifelong effort, he is in a position to dig through only a really small piece of the immense depths, and that piece will be covered over in front of his very eyes by the work of the person next to him, so that a third person would apparently do well to select a new place for the tunneling efforts he undertakes on his own initiative.

Now, if one person convincingly demonstrates that it is impossible to reach the antipodes by this direct route, who will want to continue to work on in the old depths, unless there was a possibility in the meantime that he would be happy finding some valuable rock or discovering some natural law? For that reason, Lessing, the most noble theoretical man, dared to state that for him the search for the truth counted for more than truth itself. That statement unmasks the fundamental secret of scientific knowledge, to the astonishment, even the anger, of scientists. Now, of course, alongside this single recognition, excessively truthful and brave, stands a profound but delusive image, which first came into the world in the person of Socrates, that unshakeable faith that thinking, guided by the idea of causality, might reach into the deepest abyss of being, and that thinking is capable of, not just understanding being, but even correcting it. This lofty metaphysical delusion is inherent in scientific research and leads it over and over again to its limits, at which point it must turn itself into art, something which is really predictable in this mechanical process.

With the torch of this idea, let's look at Socrates. To us he appears as the first person who was capable not only of living under the guidance of this scientific instinct, but also of dying under it (something much more difficult). Therefore the picture of the dying Socrates as a man raised above fear of death by knowledge and reason is the emblazoned shield hanging over the entranceway to scientific research, reminding every individual of his purpose, namely, to make existence intelligible and thus apparently justified. Of course, when reasoning cannot succeed in this endeavour, myth must finally serve, something which I have just noted as the necessary consequence, indeed, even the purpose of, science.

Anyone who clearly sees how, after Socrates, that mystagogue of knowledge, one philosophical school after another, like wave after wave, arose in turn, and how an unimaginable universal greed for knowledge through the full extent of the educated world steered knowledge around on the high seas as the essential task for every person of greater capabilities, a greed which it has been impossible since then completely to expel from scientific knowledge, and how through this universal greed a common net of thinking was cast over the entire earth for the first time (with even glimpses of the rule-bound workings of an entire solar system)—whoever reminds himself of all this, together with that astonishingly high pyramid of contemporary knowledge, cannot deny that in Socrates we see a turning point and vortex of so-called world history.

Imagine for a moment the following scenario: if the incalculable sum of all the energy which has been used in pursuit of this world project is spent not in the service of knowledge but on the practical (i.e., egotistical) aims of individuals and peoples, then in all probability the instinctive delight in living would be so weakened in universal wars of destruction and continuing migrations of people that, with suicide being a common occurrence, the individual, perhaps out of a sense of duty, would have to see death as a final rest and, like the inhabitants of the Fiji Islands, the son would strangle his parents, the friend would strangle his friend. A practical pessimism, which could give rise to a dreadful ethic of mass murder out of sympathy, such a belief is present and was present all over the world, wherever art did not appear in some form or other, especially in religion and science, as a remedy and a defense against that pestilence.

With respect to this practical pessimism, Socrates is the original picture of the theoretical optimist, who in the belief (which I have described) that we could discover the nature of things conferred upon knowing and discovering the power of a universal medicine and understood evil-in-itself as error. To push forward with that reasoning and to separate true knowledge from appearance and error seem to the Socratic man to be the noblest, even the single truly human vocation, just as that mechanism of ideas, judgments, and conclusions has been valued, from Socrates on, as the highest activity and the most admirable gift of nature, above all other faculties. Even the noblest moral deeds, the sympathetic emotions, self-sacrifice, heroism and that calmness in the soul (so difficult to attain), which the Apollonian Greeks called sophrosyne—all these were derived by Socrates and his like-minded descendants right up to the present from the dialectic of knowledge and therefore described as teachable.

Whoever has experienced the delight of a Socratic discovery and feels how this, in ever-widening rings, seeks to enclose the entire world of phenomena, will experience no spur capable of pushing him into existence more intense than the desire to complete that conquest and to weave a solid impenetrable net. To a man so minded, the Platonic Socrates appears as the teacher of an entirely new form of "Greek serenity" and of a blissful existence which seeks to discharge itself in actions. And these actions will consist, for the most part, like those of a mid-wife, of things concerned with the education of noble disciples, in order to produce an endless supply of geniuses.

But now science, incited by its powerful delusion, speeds on inexorably right to its limits, at which point the optimism hidden in the essence of logic fails. For the circumference of the circle of science has an infinity of points, and while it is still impossible to see how that circumference could ever be completely measured, nevertheless the noble, talented man, before the middle of his life, inevitably comes up against some border point on that circumference, where he stares at something which cannot be illuminated. When, at this point, he sees to his horror how logic turns around on itself and finally bites its own tail, then a new form of knowledge breaks through, the acknowledgement of the tragic, which in order merely to be endured, requires art as a protector and healer.

If we look at the loftiest realms of the world streaming around us, our eyes strengthened and refreshed by the Greeks, we become aware of that greed of insatiably optimistic knowledge (which Socrates previews for us) turning into tragic resignation and a need for art, even if it's true that this same greed, in its lower levels, must express itself as hostile to art and must especially loathe Dionysian tragic art, as I have already explained in the example of the conflict between Aeschylean tragedy and Socratic doctrine.

Here we are now knocking, with turbulent feelings, on the door of the present and future: Will that transformation lead to continuously new configurations of genius and straight to the music-playing Socrates? Will that wide net of art, whether in the name of religion or of science, fly over existence always more tightly and delicately, or is it determined that it will be ripped to shreds by the restless barbaric impulses and hurly-burly which we now call "the present." We are standing here on the sidelines as lookers on, worried but not without hope, for we are being permitted to witness that immense struggle and transition. Ah, but there is a magic spell in these battles: whoever looks at them must also fight them!

16

By setting out this historical example, we have attempted to clarify how tragedy surely dies away with the disappearance of the spirit of music, since tragedy can arise only out of this spirit. To mitigate the strangeness of this claim and, on the other hand, to indicate the origin of this idea of ours, we must now openly face up to analogous phenomena of the present time. We must stride right into the midst of those battles which, as I have just said, are being waged in the loftiest spheres of our present world between the insatiably optimistic desire to know and the artistic need for tragedy.

In this discussion, I shall omit all the other opposing drives which have in every age worked against art (especially against tragedy) and which at present have taken hold to such an extent that, for example, in the art of the theatre, only farces and ballets achieve a fairly rich profit with their fragrant blooms, which are perhaps not for everyone. I shall speak only of the most illustrious opposition to the tragic world view: by that I mean research scholarship, optimistic to the core of its being, with its father Socrates perched on the pinnacle. Shortly I shall also indicate by name the forces which seem to me to guarantee a new birth of tragedy and who knows what other blessed hopes for the German character!

Before we leap into the middle of this battle, let us wrap ourselves in the armour of the knowledge we seized upon earlier. In opposition to all those eager to derive art from a single principle as the necessary living origin of every work of art, I keep my eyes fixed on both those artistic divinities of the Greeks, Apollo and Dionysus, and recognize in them the living and clear representatives of two art worlds, very different in their deepest being and their highest goals. Apollo stands before me as the transfigured genius of the principium individuationis [the individualizing principle], through which release is only to be truly attained in illusion. However, under the mystical joyous cries of Dionysus, the spell of individuation shatters and the way lies open to the maternal source of being, to the innermost core of things.

This tremendous difference, which opens up a yawning gap between plastic art as Apollonian and music as Dionysian art became more or less obvious to only one great thinker, when he, without any prompting from the symbolism of the Greek gods, recognized the different character of music and the origin of all other arts from it, because music is not, like all the others art forms, images of appearances, but an immediate reflection of the will itself, and also because it presents itself as the metaphysical counterpart to all physical things in the world, the thing-in-itself as counterpart to all appearances (Schopenhauer, World as Will and Idea, I, p. 310).

On the basis of this most significant way of understanding all aesthetics, which, taken seriously, marks the first beginning of aesthetics, Richard Wagner, to confirm its lasting truth, set his stamp, when he established in his Beethoven that music must be assessed on aesthetic principles entirely different from those for all fine arts and not at all according to the category of beauty, although an erroneous aesthetics, in the service of a misleading and degenerate art, has become accustomed to the idea of beauty asserting itself in the world of images and to demand from music an effect similar to the effect of plastic arts, namely, the arousal of satisfaction in beautiful forms.

After my recognition of that tremendous opposition, I sensed in myself a strong urge to approach the essence of Greek tragedy and, in so doing, the deepest insight into the Hellenic genius. Now for the first time I believed I was capable of the magical task of posing the basic problem of tragedy in my own mind, over and above the jargon of our customary aesthetics. Through that, such an strange idiosyncratic glimpse into the Hellenic was granted to me that it had to appear to me as if our classical-Hellenistic scholarship (which is so proud of itself) had up to this point known, for the most part, only how to gloat over games with shadows and trivialities.

We may be able perhaps to touch on this original problem with the following question: What aesthetic effect arises when those separate powers of art, the Apollonian and the Dionysian, come to operate alongside each other? Or, put more briefly, what is the relationship between music and images and ideas? Richard Wagner applauded Schopenhauer on this very point for the restrained clarity and perceptiveness of his explanation. Schopenhauer spoke his views on this matter in the greatest detail in the following place (which I will quote again here in full, from World as Will and Idea, I, p. 309):

As a result of all this, we can look upon the world of appearance, or nature, and music as two different expressions of the same thing, which itself is thus the only analogy mediating between the two of them. Thus, an understanding of this thing is required in order to have insight into that analogy. Consequently, music, when considered as an expression of the world, is universal to the highest degree, something which even has a relationship with the universality of ideas, rather like the way these are related to particular things. Its universality is, however, in no way the empty universality of abstractions, but something of an entirely different kind, bound up with a thoroughly clear certainty. In this, music is like geometric figures and numbers, which are the universal forms of all possible objects of experience and applicable to them all a priori [before experience], although they are not abstract but vivid and always fixed.

All possible efforts, excitements, and expressions of the will, all those processes inside human beings, which reason subsumes under the broad negative concept of feelings, are there to express through the infinite number of possible melodies, but always in the universality of mere form, without matter, always only according to the thing-in-itself, not according to its appearance, like its innermost soul, without the body.

From these inner relationships which music has with the true essence of all things, we can also account for the fact that when an appropriate music is heard in any scene, business, action, or environment, this music appears to open up to us the most secret sense of these things, and seems to come forward as the most correct and clearest commentary on them. In the same way, for the man who surrenders himself entirely to the experience of a symphony it appears as if he saw all the possible events of life and the world drawn over into himself. Nevertheless, he cannot, if he thinks about it, perceive any similarity between that game of sounds and the things which come into his mind.

For music is, as mentioned, different from all other arts, in that it is not a portrayal of appearances, or more correctly, the adequate objectification of the will, but the unmediated portrayal of the will itself, as well as the metaphysical complement of all physical things in the world, presenting the thing-in-itself as complement to all appearances. We could, therefore, call the world the embodiment of music just as much as the embodiment of the will. And that's why it is understandable that music is capable of bringing out every painting, even every scene of real life and the world, with an immediate and higher significance and, of course, to do that all the more, the closer the analogy of its melody to the inner spirit of the given phenomenon. On this point we base the fact that we can set a poem to music as a song or as a vivid presentation in pantomime or as both in an opera. Such individual pictures of men's lives, given a foundation in the universal speech of music, are not bound to music and do not correspond with music by a compelling necessity, but they stand in relation to music as a random example to a universal idea. They present in the clarity of the real the very thing which music expresses in the universality of mere form.

For melodies are, to a certain extent, like general ideas, an abstraction from the real. For reality, the world of separate things, supplies clear phenomena, remarkable and individual things, the single case, to both the universality of ideas and the universality of melodies. Both of these universals, however, are, from a certain point of view, contrary, since ideas consist only of forms abstracted first from perception, rather like the stripped away outer skin of things, and are thus really and entirely abstractions.; whereas, music, by contrast, gives the heart of the thing, the innermost core, which comes before all particular shapes. This relationship is easily expressed properly in the language of the scholastics: ideas are the universalia post rem (universals after the fact); music, however, gives the universalia ante rem (universals before the fact), and reality the universalia in re (universals in the fact).

The fact that in general there can be a connection between a musical composition and a perceptible presentation rests on the point that, as stated, both are only very different expressions of same inner essence of the world. Now, when in a particular case such a connection is truly present and the composer has known how to express in the universal language of music the dynamics of the will, which constitutes the core of the event, then the melody of the song, the music of the opera, is full of expression. The composer's discovery of the analogy between both must, however, issue from the immediate realization of the world essence, unknown to his reason, and must not be an imitation, conveyed in ideas with conscious intentionality. Otherwise the music does not express the inner essence, that is, the will itself, but only imitates inadequately its appearance."

Following what Schopenhauer has taught, we also understand music as the language of the unmediated will and feel our imaginations stirred to shape that spirit world which speaks to us invisibly and nonetheless in such a vital manner and to embody it in ourselves through a metaphorical illustration. By contrast, image and idea, under the influence of a truly appropriate music, reach an elevated significance. Thus, Dionysian art customarily works in two ways on Apollonian artistic potential: music arouses us to consider an image, in some way similar to the Dionysian universality, and music then permits that image to come forward with the highest significance.

The Birth of Tragedy out of the Spirit of Music 73

From this intelligible observation and without any deeper considerations of unapproachable things, I conclude that music is capable of generating myth (that is the most meaningful example) and, indeed, of giving birth to the tragic myth, that myth which speaks of the recognition of the Dionysian among the Greeks. I have explained the phenomenon of the lyric poet, and after that how music in the lyric poet strives to make known its essence in Apollonian pictures. Let us now imagine that music at its highest intensity also must seek to reach its highest representation. Thus, we must consider it possible that music also knows how to find the symbolic expression for its essentially Dionysian wisdom. And where else will we have to look for this expression, if not in tragedy and in the idea of tragedy generally?

From the essence of art as it is commonly understood according to the single categories of illusion and beauty it is genuinely impossible to derive the tragic. Only with reference to the spirit of music do we understand a joy in the destruction of the individual. Now, individual examples of such a destruction makes clear the eternal phenomenon of Dionysian art, which brings into expression the will in its omnipotence out from behind, so to speak, the principium individuationis, the life beyond all appearances and eternal life, in spite of all destruction.

The metaphysical joy in the tragic is a translation of the instinctive unconscious Dionysian wisdom into the language of the image. The hero, the highest manifestation of the will, is destroyed, and we are happy at that, because, after all, he is only an illusion, and the eternal life of the will is not disturbed by his destruction. "We believe in eternal life," so tragedy calls out, while the music is the unmediated idea of this life. The work of the plastic artist has an entirely different purpose: Here Apollo overcomes the suffering of the individual through the bright exaltation in the eternity of the illusion. Here beauty is victorious over the suffering inherent in life. The pain is, in a certain sense, brushed away from the face of nature. In Dionysian art and in its tragic symbolism this same nature speaks to us with its true, undisguised voice: "Be as I am! Under the incessantly changing phenomena the eternal primordial mother, always forcing things into existence, always satisfied with the changing nature of appearances!"

17

Dionysian art also wants to convince us of the eternal delight in existence. But we must seek this delight, not in appearances, but behind them. We must recognize how everything which comes into being must be ready for a painful destruction. We are forced to gaze directly into the terror of individual existence but, in the process, must not become paralyzed. A metaphysical consolation tears us momentarily out of the hustle and bustle of changing forms. For a short time we really are the primordial essence itself and feel its unbridled lust for and joy in existence. The struggle, torment, and destruction of appearances we now consider necessary, on account of the excess of countless forms of existence forcefully thrusting themselves into life, and of the exuberant fecundity of the world's will. We are transfixed by the raging barbs of this torment in the very moment when we become, as it were, one with the immeasurable primordial delight in existence and when we sense the indestructible and eternal nature of this Dionysian joy. In spite of fear and compassion, we are fortunate vital beings, not as individuals, but as the one force of Life, with whose procreative joy we have been fused.

The story of how Greek tragedy arose tells us now with clear certainty how the Greeks' tragic work of art really was born out of the spirit of music. With this idea we think we have, for the first time, reached a true understanding of the original and astonishing meaning of the chorus. At the same time, however, we must concede that the significance of the tragic myth explained previously, to say nothing of Greek philosophy, was never entirely clear to the Greek poets. Their heroes speak to a certain extent more superficially than they act, and the myth does not really find its adequate objectification in the spoken word.

The structure of the scenes and the vivid images reveal a deeper wisdom than the poet himself can grasp in words and ideas. We can make the same observation about Shakespeare, whose Hamlet, for example, similarly speaks in a more superficial manner than he acts, so that we derive the above mentioned study of Hamlet, not from the words, but from the deepest view and review of the totality of the work. With respect to Greek tragedy, which, of course, comes to us only as a drama of words, I have even suggested that that incongruity between myth and word can easily seduce us into considering it shallower and more empty of meaning than it is, and thus to assume a more superficial action than it must have had according to the testimony of the ancients. For we easily forget that what the poet as a wordsmith could not achieve, the attainment of the highest intellectualization and idealization of myth, he could achieve successfully at any time as a creating musician.

Admittedly through scholarship we must recreate the extraordinary power of the musical effects in order to receive something of that incomparable consolation necessarily characteristic of true tragedy. But we would experience this extraordinary musical power for what it is only if we were Greeks, because considering the entire development of Greek music, which is well known, quite familiar to us, and infinitely richer by comparison, we believe we are hearing only youthful songs, sung with only a timid sense of their power. The Greeks are, as the Egyptian priests say, eternal children, and where tragic art is concerned, only children who do not know what an exalted toy has arisen under their hands, something which will be destroyed.

Every struggle of the spirit of music for pictorial and mythic revelation, which becomes increasingly intense from the beginning of the lyric right up to Attic tragedy, suddenly breaks apart, right after developing in full luxuriant bloom, and, so to speak, disappears from the surface of Hellenic art, although the Dionysian world view born out of this struggle lives on in the mysteries and in its most amazing transformations and degeneration never stops attracting serious natures to it. Isn't it possible that it will rise from its mystical depths as art once more?

At this point we are concerned with the question whether the power whose hostile effects broke tragedy has sufficient power for all time to hinder the artistic re-growth of tragedy and the tragic world view. If the old tragedy was derailed by the dialectical drive for knowledge and by the optimism of scholarly research, we might have to infer from this fact an eternal struggle between the theoretical and the tragic world views. And only after the spirit of knowledge is taken right to its limits and its claim to universal validity destroyed by the establishment of that limit would it be possible to hope for a re-birth of tragedy. For a symbol of such a cultural form, we would have to set up Socrates the player of music, in the sense talked about earlier. By this opposition I understand with respect to the spirit of scholarly research the belief (which first came to light in the person of Socrates) that our understanding of nature can be grounded and that knowledge has a universal healing power.

Whoever remembers the most immediate consequences of this restless forward driving spirit of scientific knowledge will immediately recall how it destroyed myth and how through this destruction poetry was driven out of its naturally ideal soil as something from now on without a home. If we have correctly ascribed to music the power to bring about out of itself a re-birth of myth, then we will have to seek out the spirit of science on that very path where it has its hostile encounter with the myth-creating power of music. This occurred in the development of the new Attic dithyramb, whose music no longer expressed the inner essence, the will itself, but only gave back an inadequate appearance in an imitation delivered through ideas. From such innerly degenerate music those with a true musical nature turned away with the same aversion which they had displayed before the art-killing tendency of Socrates.

The instinct of Aristophanes (which grasped issues so surely) was certainly right when he linked together Socrates himself, the tragedies of Euripides, and the music of the new writers of dithyrambs, hating each of them and smelling in all three of them the characteristics of a degenerate culture. Through that new dithyramb, music is criminally turned into a mimetic demonstration of appearances, for example, a battle or storm at sea, and in the process is totally robbed of all its power to create myths. For when music seeks only to arouse our indulgence by compelling us to find external analogies between an event in life or nature and certain rhythmic figures and characteristic musical sounds, when our understanding is supposed to be satisfied with the recognition of these analogies, then we are dragged down into a mood in which a conception of the mythic is impossible. For myth must be vividly felt as a single instance of universality and truth staring into the infinite.

Truly Dionysian music works on us as a universal mirror reflecting the will of the world. Each vivid event reflected in this mirror widens out at once for our feelings into the image of an eternal truth. By contrast, the sound painting of the new dithyramb immediately strips such a vivid event of its mythic character. Now the music has become a feeble copy of a phenomenon and, in the process, infinitely poorer than the phenomenon itself. Through this impoverishment the phenomenon itself is even lowered in our feelings, so that now, for example, a battle imitated in this kind of music plays itself feebly out in marches, trumpet calls, and so forth, and our imagination is held back precisely by these superficialities.

Painting with music is thus in every respect the opposite to the myth creating power of true music. Through the former a phenomenon becomes more impoverished than it is, whereas through Dionysian music the individual phenomenon becomes richer and widens into an image of the world. It was a powerful victory of the non-Dionysian spirit when, in the development of the new dithyramb, it alienated music from itself and pushed it down to be the slave of appearances. Euripides, who, in a higher sense, must have had a thoroughly unmusical nature, is for this very reason an ardent supporter of the new dithyrambic music and uses all its stock effects and styles with the open-handedness of a thief.

From another perspective we see the force of this un-Dionysian spirit in action directing its effects against myth, when we turn our gaze toward the way in which the presentation of character and the psychological complexities get way out of hand in the tragedies of Sophocles. The character cannot be allowed to broaden out any more into an eternal type, but, by contrast, must appear an individual through the artistic qualifications and shading, through the most delicate clarity of every line, so that the spectator generally no longer experiences the myth but the commanding naturalism of the artist, his power of imitation.

Here also we become aware of the victory of appearances over the universal and of the delight in the particular, rather like an anatomical specimen. Already we breathe the air of a theoretical world, which values the scientific insight higher than the artistic mirror image of a universal principle. The movement along the line of increasing characterization quickly goes further. While Sophocles still paints whole characters and yokes their sophisticated development to myth, Euripides already paints only large individual character traits, which are capable of expressing themselves in violent passions. In the new Attic comedy there are masks with only one expression, reckless old men, deceived pimps, mischievous slaves in an inexhaustible repetition.

Where now has the myth-building spirit of music gone? What is left now for music is music of stimulation or memory, that is, either music as a means of stimulating jaded and worn out nerves or sound painting. As far as the first is concerned, the text is largely irrelevant. Already in Euripides, when his heroes or chorus first start to sing, things get really out of hand. What must it have been like with his unapologetic successors?

However, the new un-Dionysian spirit manifests itself with the utmost clarity in the conclusions of the new plays. In the old tragedy, the metaphysical consolation was there to feel at the conclusion. Without that, the delight in tragedy simply cannot be explained. The sound of reconciliation from another world echoes most purely perhaps in Oedipus at Colonus. But as soon as the genius of music flew away from tragedy, tragedy is, in the strong sense of the term, dead. For out of what are people now able to create that metaphysical consolation?

Consequently, people looked for an earthly solution to tragic dissonance. After the hero was sufficiently tortured by fate, he was paid a well earned reward in an impressive marriage, in divine testament to his honour. The hero became a gladiator, to whom people gave his freedom, after he had been well beaten and was covered with wounds. The deus ex machina moved in to take the place of metaphysical consolation. I will not say that the tragic world view was destroyed entirely and completely by the surging spirit of the un-Dionysian. We only know that it must have fled out of art as if into the underworld, degenerating into a secret cult.

But over the widest surface area of Hellenistic existence raged the consuming wind of that spirit which announces itself in the form of "Greek serenity," to which I referred earlier as an impotent and unproductive delight in life. This serenity is a counterpart to the marvelous "naïveté" of the old Greeks, which we must see—in accordance with its given characteristics—as the flowering of Apollonian culture, blossoming out of a dark abyss, as the victory over suffering, the wisdom of suffering, which the Hellenic will gains through its ability to mirror beauty.

The noblest form of that other form of "Greek serenity," the Alexandrian, is the cheerfulness of the theoretical man. It manifests the same characteristic features I already derived out of the idea of the un-Dionysian: it fights against Dionysian wisdom and art; it strives to dissolve myth; it places an earthy consonance in place of a metaphysical consolation, indeed a particular deus ex machina, namely, the god of machines and crucibles, that is, the force of nature, recognized and used in the service of a higher egoism; it believes in correcting the world through knowledge, a life led by scientific knowledge, and thus is really in a position to confine the individual man in the narrowest circle of problems which can be solved, inside which he can cheerfully say to life: "I want you. You are worth knowing."

18

It's an eternal phenomenon: the voracious will always finds a way to keep its creatures alive and force them on to further living by an illusion spread over things. One man is fascinated by the Socratic desire for knowledge and the delusion that with it he'll be able to cure the eternal wound of existence. Another is caught up by the seductively beautiful veil of art fluttering before his eyes; yet another by the metaphysical consolation that underneath the hurly-burly of appearances eternal life flows on indestructibly, to say nothing of the more common and almost more powerful illusions which the will holds ready at all times. In general, these three stages of illusion are only for nobly endowed natures, those who feel the weight and difficulty of existence with more profound reluctance and who need to be deceived out of this reluctance by these exquisite stimulants. Everything we call culture emerges from these stimulants: depending on the proportions of the mixture we have a predominantly Socratic or artistic or tragic culture—or if you'll permit historical examples—there is either an Alexandrian or a Hellenic or a Buddhist culture.

Our entire modern world is trapped in the net of Alexandrian culture and recognizes as its ideal the theoretical man, equipped with the highest intellectual powers and working in the service of science, a man for whom Socrates is the prototype and progenitor. All our methods of education originally have this ideal in view. Every other existence has struggled on with difficulty alongside this ideal as a way of life we permit, not as one we intend. For a long time now, it's been almost frightening to sense how an educated person here is found only in the form of the scholar. Even our literary arts have had to develop out of scholarly imitations, and in the main effect of rhyme we recognize still the development of our poetical form out of artificial experiments with what is essentially really a scholarly language, not one native to us.

To a true Greek how incomprehensible must Faust have appeared, that man of modern culture, who is inherently intelligible to us—Faust, who storms dissatisfied through all faculties, his drive for knowledge making him devoted to magic and the devil. We have only to stand him beside Socrates for comparison in order to recognize that modern man is beginning to have a premonition of the limits of that Socratic desire for knowledge and is yearning for a coastline somewhere in the wide and desolate sea of knowledge. When Goethe once remarked to Eckermann, with reference to Napoleon, "Yes, my good man, there is also a productivity in actions," in a delightfully naïve way he was reminding us that the non-theoretical human being is something implausible and astonishing to modern man, so that we had to have the wisdom of a Goethe to find out that such a strange form of existence is comprehensible, even forgivable.

And now we must not conceal from ourselves what lies hidden in the womb of this Socratic culture! An optimism that thinks itself all powerful! Well, people should not be surprised when the fruits of this optimism ripen, when a society that has been thoroughly leavened with this kind of culture, right down to the lowest levels, gradually starts trembling in an extravagant turmoil of desires, when the belief in earthly happiness for everyone, when faith in the possibility of such a universal knowledge culture gradually changes into the threatening demand for such an Alexandrian earthly happiness, into the invocation of a Euripidean deus ex machina!

People should take note: Alexandrian culture requires a slave class in order to be able to exist over time, but with its optimistic view of existence, it denies the necessity for such a class and thus, when the effect of its beautiful words of seduction and reassurance about the "dignity of human beings" and the "dignity of work" has worn off, it gradually moves towards a horrific destruction. There is nothing more frightening than a barbarian slave class which has learned to think of its existence as an injustice and is preparing to take revenge, not only for itself, but for all generations.

In the face of such threatening storms, who dares appeal with sure confidence to our pale and exhausted religions, which themselves in their foundations have degenerated into scholarly religions, so that myth, the essential precondition for all religions, is already everywhere paralyzed—even in this area that optimistic spirit which we have just described as the germ of destruction of our society has gained control.

While the disaster slumbering in the bosom of theoretical culture gradually begins to worry modern man and while he, in his uneasiness, reaches into the treasure of his experience for ways to avert the danger, without any inherent faith in these means, and while he also begins to have a premonition of his own particular consequences, some great and widely gifted natures have, with incredibly careful thought, known how to use the tools of science to set out the boundaries and relative nature of knowledge itself and, in the process, decisively to deny the claim of science to universal validity and universal goals. With proofs like this, for the first time that delusion which presumes with the help of causality to be able to ground the innermost essence of things has become recognized for what it is.

The immense courage and wisdom of Kant and Schopenhauer achieved the most difficult victory, the one over the optimism lying concealed in the essential nature of logic, which is, in turn, the foundation of our culture. While this logic, based on aeternae veritates [eternal truths] which it did not consider open to objection, had believed that all the riddles of the world could be recognized and resolved and had treated space, time, and causality as totally unconditional laws with the most universal validity, Kant showed how these really served only to raise mere appearance, the work of Maja, to the only reality, the highest reality, and to set it in place as the innermost and true essence of things and thus to make true knowledge of this essence impossible, that is, to use an expression of

Schopenhauer, to get the dreamer to sleep even more soundly (World as Will and Idea, I, 498).

With this recognition there is introduced a culture which I venture to describe as a tragic culture. Its most important distinguishing feature is that wisdom replaces knowledge as the highest goal, a wisdom which, undeceived by the seductive diversions of science, turns its unswerving gaze towards the all-encompassing picture of the world and, with a sympathetic feeling of love, seeks in that world to grasp eternal suffering as its own suffering. Let's imagine a growing generation with this fearless gaze, this heroic attraction for what is immense; let's imagine the bold step of these dragon slayers, the proud daring with which they turn their backs on all the doctrines of weakness belonging to that optimism, in order to "live resolutely," fully and completely. Would that not require the tragic man of this culture in his self-education for seriousness and terror to desire a new art, the art of metaphysical consolation, to desire tragedy as the Helen which belongs to him and to have to cry out with Faust:

With my desire's power, should I not call Into this life the fairest form of all?

However, now that Socratic culture has been shaken on two sides—once by the fear of its own consequences, which it is definitely beginning to sense, and, in addition, because it is itself no longer convinced of the eternal validity of its foundations with that earlier naïve trust—it can hang onto the sceptre of its infallibility only with trembling hands. So it's a sorry spectacle—how the dance of its thinking dashes longingly after new forms in order to embrace them and then how, like Mephistopheles with the seductive Lamia, it suddenly, with a shudder, lets them go.

That is, in fact, the characteristic mark of that fracture which everyone habitually talks about as the root malady of modern culture, that theoretical man is afraid of his own consequences and, in his dissatisfaction, no longer dares to commit himself to the fearful ice currents of existence. He runs anxiously up and down along the shore. He no longer wants to have anything completely, any totality with all the natural cruelty of things. That's how much the optimistic way of seeing things has mollycoddled him. At the same time he feels how a culture which has been built on the principles of science must collapse when it begins to become illogical, that is, when it begins to run back, away from its own consequences.

Our art reveals this general distress: in vain people use imitation to lean on all the great productive periods and natures; in vain they gather all "world literature" around modern man to bring him consolation and place him in the middle of artistic styles and artists of all ages, so that he may, like Adam with the animals, give them a name. But he remains an eternally hungry man, the "critic" without joy and power, the Alexandrian man, who is basically a librarian and copy editor and goes miserably blind from the dust of books and printing errors.

19

We can designate the innermost form of this Socratic culture most precisely when we call it the culture of opera, for in this area our Socratic culture, with characteristic naiveté, has expressed its wishes and perceptions—something astonishing to us if we bring the genesis of opera and the facts of the development of opera together with the eternal truths of the Apollonian and the Dionysian.

First, I recall the emergence of the stilo rappresentativo [the representational style] and of recitative. Is it credible that this entirely externalized opera music, something incapable of worship, could be accepted and preserved with wildly enthusiastic favour, as if it were the rebirth of all true music, in an age in which Palestrina's inexpressibly awe-inspiring and sacred music had just arisen? On the other hand, who would make the diversion-loving voluptuousness of those Florentine circles or the vanity of its dramatic singers responsible for such a rapidly spreading love of opera? The fact that in the same age, indeed, in the same peoples, alongside the vaulted structure of Palestrina's harmonies, which the entire Christian Middle Ages had developed, there awoke that passion for a half-musical way of speaking—that I can only explain by some tendency beyond art, something also at work in the very nature of recitative.

To the listener who wishes to hear clearly the word under the singing, there corresponds the singer who speaks more than he sings and who intensifies the expressions of pathos in half-singing. Through this intensification of pathos he makes the words easier to understand

and overpowers what's left of the musical half. The real danger now threatening him is that at an inopportune moment he may give the music the major emphasis, so that the pathos in the speech and the clarity of the words necessarily disappear. On the other hand, he always feels the urge for musical release and a virtuoso presentation of his voice. Here the "poet" comes to his assistance, the man who knows how to provide him sufficient opportunities for lyrical interjections, repetitions of words and sentences, and so on, places where the singer can now rest in a purely musical element, without considering the words. This alternation of only half-sung speech full of urgent emotion and interjections which are all singing, which lies at the heart of the stilo rappresentativo, this rapidly changing effort at one moment to affect the understanding and imagination of the listener and at another to work on his musical senses, is something so completely unnatural and at the same time so innerly contradictory to the Dionysian and Apollonian artistic drives that we must conclude that the origin of recitative lies outside all artistic instincts.

According to this account, we should define recitative as the mixing of epic and lyric performing, but not at all in an innerly consistent blending, which could never have been attained with such entirely disparate things, but the most external conglutination, in the style of a mosaic, something the like of which has no model whatsoever in the realm of nature and experience. But this was not the opinion of those inventors of recitative. Rather they—along with their age—believed that through that stilo rappresentativo the secret of ancient music had been resolved and that only through it could one explain the tremendous effect of an Orpheus, Amphion, and, indeed, even of Greek tragedy. The new style was valued as the re-awakening of the most effective music—the music of the ancient Greeks. In fact, under the universal and totally popular conception of the Homeric world as the primitive world, people allowed themselves to surrender to the dream that they had now climbed down back once more into the paradisal beginnings of humankind, when music necessarily must have had that superb purity, power, and innocence which the poets knew how to talk about so movingly in their pastoral plays.

Here we see the innermost development of this truly modern style of art, the opera. A powerful need forces itself out in art, but it is a need of an unaesthetic sort: the yearning for the idyllic, the belief in a primordial existence of the artistic and good man. Recitative served as the rediscovered language of that primordial man, and opera as the rediscovered land of that idyllic or heroically good being, who in all his actions at the same time follows a natural artistic drive, who sings at least something in everything he has to say, so that, given the slightest emotional arousal, he can immediately sing out in full voice.

For us now it is unimportant that contemporary humanists used this newly created picture of the paradisal artist to fight against the old church idea of human beings as inherently corrupt and lost, so that opera is to be understood as the opposing dogma of good people, something in which they simultaneously discovered a way of consoling themselves against that pessimism to which the seriously minded people of that time, given the horrifying uncertainties of all social conditions, were attracted most strongly. It's enough for us to recognize how the real magic and thus the origin of this new artistic form lies in the satisfaction of an entirely unaesthetic need, in the optimistic glorification of man as such, in its view of primitive man as naturally good and artistic man. This operatic principle has gradually transformed itself into a threatening and terrible demand, which we, faced with the socialist movement of the present day, can no longer fail to hear. The "good primitive man" wants his rights: what paradisal prospects!

Alongside this point I set another equally clear confirmation of my opinion that opera is constructed on the same principles as our Alexandrian culture. Opera is the birth of theoretical man, of the critical layman, not of the artist—one of the strangest facts in the history of all the arts. It was the demand of completely unmusical listeners that people had to hear the words above all, so that a rebirth of music was only to be expected when some way of singing was discovered according to which the words of the text rule over the counterpoint the way a lord rules his servants. For the words (they said) are nobler than the accompanying harmonic system just as the soul is nobler than the body. In the beginning of opera, the union of music, image, and word was treated according to the amateurish and unmusical crudity of these views. The first experiments with the sense of this aesthetic were launched in distinguished amateur circles in Florence by the poets and singers patronized there.

The man who is artistically impotent produces for himself a form of art precisely because he is the inherently inartistic man. Because he has no sense of the Dionysian depths of music, for his own sake he transforms musical taste into easy to understand verbal and musical rhetoric of the passions in stilo rappresentativo and into the voluptuousness of the art of singing. Because he is incapable of seeing a vision, he presses mechanics and decorative artists into his service. Because he has no idea how to grasp the true essence of the artist, he conjures up right in front of him the "artistic primitive man" to suit his own taste, that is, the man who, when passionate, sings and speaks verse. He dreams himself back in an age in which passion was sufficient to produce songs and poems, as if that feeling has ever been in a position to create something artistic. The precondition of opera is a false belief about the artistic process; it is, in fact, the idyllic faith that in reality every sensitive man is an artist. According to the meaning of this belief, opera is the expression of lay amateurs in art, something which dictates its laws with the cheerful optimism of theoretical man.

If we wanted to bring together into a single conception both of these ideas I have just described in connection with the origin of opera, all we would have left to do is to speak of an idyllic tendency in opera—and the only things we would need to use are Schiller's way of expressing himself and his explanation. He claimed that nature and the ideal are either an object of sorrow, when the former is represented as lost and the latter as unattained or both are an object of joy, when they are represented as real. The first produces the elegy in a narrower sense, and the other produces the idyll in its broadest sense. And right away we must draw attention to the common characteristic of both of these ideas in the genesis of opera—that in them the ideal does not register as unattained and nature does not register as lost.

According to this feeling, there was a primordial time for man when he lay on the heart of nature and, with this state of nature, simultaneously attained the ideal of humanity in paradisal goodness and artistry. We all are said to have descended from these perfect primitive men, indeed, we still were their faithful image—we only had to cast some things away from us in order to recognize ourselves once again as these primitive people, thanks to a voluntary renunciation of superfluous scholarship, of lavish culture.

Through his operatic imitation of Greek tragedy, the educated man of the Renaissance let himself be led back to such a harmony of nature and the ideal, to an idyllic reality. He used this tragedy, as Dante used Virgil, to be brought right up to the gates of paradise, while from this point on he strode even further on his own and passed over from an imitation of the highest Greek art form to a "restoration of all things," to a copy of man's original art world.

What a confident good nature there is in these audacious attempts, right in the bosom of theoretical culture! Something to be explained only by the comforting faith that "man in himself" is the eternally virtuous hero of opera, the eternally piping or singing shepherd, who must always in the end rediscover himself as such, should he find out at some time or other that he has really lost himself for a while—something which is only the fruit of that optimism which here arises out of the depths of the Socratic world view, like a sweetly seductive fragrant column of air.

Hence among the characteristics of opera there is no sense at all of that elegiac pain of eternal loss—there is rather the cheerfulness of an eternal rediscovery, the comfortable joy in an idyllic reality which man can at least imagine for himself at all times. But in doing this, man may perhaps at some point suspect that this imagined reality is nothing other than a fantastically silly indulgence. Anyone able to measure this against the fearful seriousness of true nature and to compare it with the actual primitive scenes of the beginnings of humanity would have to cry out in disgust—Get rid of that phantom!

Nevertheless, we would be deceiving ourselves if we believed that such a playful being as opera could be chased away simply by a powerful shout, like a ghost. Whoever wants to destroy opera must undertake the struggle against that Alexandrine cheerfulness which expresses its favourite idea so naively in opera; in fact, opera is its real artistic form. But what can we expect for art itself from the effect of a form of art whose origins in general do not lie in the aesthetic realm but which have rather stolen from a half moralistic sphere over into the realm of art and which can deceive people about its hybrid origin only now and then?

On what juices does this parasitic operatic being feed itself, if not from the sap of true art? Are we not to assume that, under the influence of opera's idyllic seductions and its Alexandrine arts of flattering, the highest task of art, the one we should take really seriously—saving the eye from a glimpse into the horror of the night and through the healing balm of illusion rescuing the subject from the spasms brought about by the strivings of the will—would degenerate into a trend to empty and scattered diversion? What happens to the eternal truths of the Dionysian and the Apollonian in such a mixture of styles of the sort I have set down as the essence of the stilo rappresentativo, where the music is considered the servant and the libretto the master, where the music is compared to the body and the libretto to the soul, where the highest goal at best will aim at a descriptive tone painting, as it was earlier with the new Attic dithyramb, where the music is completely alienated from its true office, which is to be a Dionysian world-mirror, so that the only thing left for it is to imitate the essential forms of appearances, like a slave of phenomena, and to arouse superficial entertainment in the play of lines and proportions?

A rigorous examination shows how this fatal influence of opera on music coincides precisely with the entire development of modern music. The optimism lurking in the genesis of opera and in the essence of the culture represented through opera succeeded with alarming speed in stripping music of its Dionysian world meaning and stamping on it a formally playful and entertaining character. This transformation can only be compared to something like the metamorphosis of Aeschylean man into the Alexandrian cheerful man.

If in the explanation given above we have been right to link the disappearance of the Dionysian spirit with an extremely striking but so far unexplained transformation and degeneration of Greek man, what hopes must revive in us when the most certain favourable signs bring us the guarantee of the gradual awakening of the Dionysian spirit in our contemporary world! It is not possible that the divine power of Hercules should remain always impotent in voluptuous bondage to Omphale. Out of the Dionysian foundation of the German spirit a power has arisen which has nothing in common with the most basic assumptions of Socratic culture, something those assumptions cannot explain or excuse. Rather from the point of view of this culture it is experienced as something terrible which cannot be explained, as something overpoweringly hostile—and that is German music, above all as it is to be understood in its forceful orbit from Bach to Beethoven, from Beethoven to Wagner.

Even in the best of circumstances what can the Socratic man of our day, greedy for knowledge, begin to make of this daemon rising from the inexhaustible depths? Neither from the lacework or arabesques of operatic melodies nor with the help of the arithmetic abacus of fugue and contrapuntal dialectic will a formula reveal itself in whose triple-powered light people can render that daemon obsequious and compel it to speak. What a spectacle when our aestheticians nowadays, with the fishing net of "beauty" all their own, strike at and try to catch that musical genius roaming about in front of them with incredible life, with movements which will not be judged according to eternal beauty any more than according to notions of the sublime. We should only inspect these patrons of music in person and at close quarters, when they cry out so tirelessly "Beauty! Beauty!" to see whether they look like educated and discriminating darling children of nature or whether they are not rather seeking a deceptively euphemistic form for their own crudity, an aesthetic pretext for their characteristically unfeeling sobriety. Here, for example, I'm thinking of Otto Jahn.

But the liar and hypocrite should beware of German music, for in the midst of all our culture it is precisely the one unalloyed pure and purifying fire spirit out from which and towards which all things move in a double orbit, as in the doctrine of the great Heraclitus of Ephesus: everything which we now call culture, education, and civilization must at some point appear before the unerring judge Dionysus. Furthermore, let's remember how the spirit of German philosophy in Kant and Schopenhauer, streaming from the same springs, was able to annihilate the contented joy in existence of scholarly Socratism by demonstrating its boundaries, and how with this demonstration an infinitely deeper and more serious consideration of ethical questions and art was introduced, which we can truly describe as Dionysian wisdom conceptually understood.

Where does the mystery of this unity between German music and German philosophy point if not to a new form of existence, about whose meaning we can inform ourselves only by speculating on the basis of analogies with the Greeks? For the Greek model has this immeasurable value for us who stand on the border line between two different forms of existence—that in it are stamped all those transitions and struggles in a classically instructive form, except that we are, as it were, living through the great high points of Greek being in the reverse order. For example, we seem to be moving now out of an Alexandrian period backwards into a period of tragedy.

At the same time, we feel as if the birth of a tragic time period for the German spirit only means a return to itself, a blessed re-discovery of self, after immensely powerful forces from outside had for a long time forced it into servitude under their form, since that spirit, so far as form is concerned, lived in helpless barbarism. And now finally after its return home to the original spring of its being, it can dare to stride in here before all peoples, bold and free, without the guiding reins of Roman civilization. If only it can now understand how to learn all the time from a single people, the Greeks—being capable of learning from them is already a high honour and a remarkable distinction. And when have we needed these most eminent of mentors more than now, when we are experiencing the rebirth of tragedy and are in danger of not knowing where it is coming from or of being able to interpret where it is going?

20

At some point under the gaze of an incorruptible judge we may determine in what ages and in which men up to now the German spirit has struggled most powerfully to learn from the Greeks. And if we can assume with some confidence that this extraordinary praise must be awarded to the noblest cultural struggles of Goethe, Schiller, and Winckelmann, then we would certainly have to add that since that time and the most recent developments of that battle, the attempt to attain a culture and to reach the Greeks by the same route has become incomprehensibly weaker and weaker.

In order to avoid being forced into total despair about the German spirit, shouldn't we conclude from all this that in some important point or other these fighters were not successful in penetrating the Hellenic spirit and creating a lasting bond of love between German and Greek culture? And beyond that, perhaps an unconscious recognition of this failure gives rise in serious people to the enervating doubt whether, after such predecessors, they could go even further than these men had along this cultural path and reach their goal at all. For that reason since that time we've seen judgments about the educational value of the Greeks degenerate in the most disturbing way. We can hear expressions of sympathetic condescension in the most varied encampments of the spirit and of the lack of spirit. In other places a completely ineffectual sweet talk flirts with "Greek harmony," "Greek beauty," and "Greek cheerfulness."

And precisely in the circles which could dignify themselves by drawing tirelessly from the Greek river bed in order to benefit German education—the circles of teachers in the institutes of higher education—people have learned best to come to terms with the Greeks early and in a comfortable manner, often with a sceptical abandoning of the Hellenic ideal and a total reversal of the real purpose of classical studies. In general, anyone in these circles who hasn't completely exhausted himself in the effort to be a dependable corrector of old texts or a microscopic studier of language, like some natural historian may perhaps also seek to acquire Greek antiquity "historically," as well as other antiquities, but in any case following the methods of our present scholarly writing, along with their supercilious expressions.

If, as a result, the real cultural power of our institutions of higher learning has certainly never been lower and weaker than at present, if the "journalist," the paper slave of the day, has won his victory over the professors so far as culture is concerned and the only thing still left for the latter is the frequently experienced metamorphosis which has them also moving around these days with the speech styles of a journalist, with the "light elegance" of this sphere, like cheerful well-educated butterflies, then how awkward and confusing it must be for people living in such a present and educated in this manner to stare at that phenomenon of the revival of the Dionysian spirit and the rebirth of tragedy, something which may only be understood by some analogy to the most profound principles of the as yet incomprehensible Hellenic genius.

There is no other artistic period in which so-called culture and true art have stood more alienated from and averse to each other than what we witness with our own eyes nowadays. We understand why such a weak culture despises true art, for it fears such art will destroy it. But surely an entire form of culture, i.e., the Socratic-Alexandrian, must have run its full life after being able to culminate in such a delicate and insignificant point as our present culture.

When heroes like Schiller and Goethe couldn't succeed in breaking down that enchanted door which leads to the Hellenic magic mountain, when for all their most courageous struggles they reached no further than that yearning gaze which Goethe's Iphigeneia sent from barbaric Tauris over the sea towards her home, what is left for the imitators of such heroes to hope for, unless from some totally different side, untouched by all the efforts of previous culture, the door might suddenly open on its own—to the accompaniment of the mysterious sound of the reawakened music of tragedy.

Let no one try to detract from our belief in a still imminent rebirth of Hellenic antiquity, for that's the only place where we find our hope for a renewal and reformation of the German spirit through the fiery magic of music. What would we otherwise know to name which amid the desolation and weariness of contemporary culture could awaken some comforting expectation for the future? We look in vain for a single powerfully branching root, for a spot of fertile and healthy soil—but everywhere there is dust, sand, ossification, and decay. Here a desperate, isolated man couldn't choose a better symbol than the knight with Death and the Devil, as Dürer has drawn him for us, the knight in armour with the hard bronze gaze, who knows how to make his way along his terrible path, without wavering at his horrific companions—and yet without any hope, alone with his horse and hound. Such a Dürer knight was our Schopenhauer: he lacked all hope, but he wanted the truth. There is no one like him.

But how suddenly that wilderness of such an exhausted culture as the one I have just sketched out so gloomily changes when the Dionysian magic touches it! A tempest seizes everything worn out, rotten, broken apart, and stunted, wraps it in a red whirling cloud of dust, and lifts it like a vulture up into the air. In our bewilderment, our gaze seeks out what has disappeared, for what we see has risen up as if from oblivion into golden light, so full and green, so richly alive, so immeasurable and full of longing. Tragedy sits in the midst of this superfluity of life, suffering, and joy; with awe-inspiring delight it listens to a distant melancholy song, which tells of the mothers of being whose names are Delusion, Will, and Woe.

Yes, my friends, believe with me in the Dionysian life and in the rebirth of tragedy. The age of the Socratic man is over: crown yourselves with ivy, take the thyrsus stalk in your hand, and don't be amazed when tigers and panthers lie down fawning at your feet. Only now you must dare to be tragic men, for you will be redeemed. You are to lead the Dionysian celebratory procession from India to Greece! Arm yourselves for a hard battle, but have faith in the miracles of your god!

21

Moving back from this tone of exhortation into a mood suitable for contemplation, I repeat that only from the Greeks can we learn what such a miraculously sudden awakening of tragedy can mean for the innermost fundamental life of a people. It is the people of tragic mystery who fight the Persian wars, and again the people who carried on these wars uses tragedy as an essential potion in their recovery. Who would have supposed that such a people, after being stirred right to their innermost being for several generations by the strongest paroxysms of the Dionysian demon, were still capable of a regular and powerful outpouring of the simplest political feeling, the most natural instinctive feeling for their homeland, the original manly desire to fight?

Nonetheless, if we always sense in that remarkable extension of oneself into one's surroundings associated with Dionysian arousal how Dionysian release from the shackles of individuality registers at first as a heightened indifference—even apathy and hostility—to the political instincts, on the other hand, Apollo, the nation builder, is also the genius of the principium individuationis [individualizing principle], and a sense of state and homeland cannot survive without an affirmation of the individual personality.

From ecstatic experience there is only one way out for a people, the route to Indian Buddhism, which, with its longing for nothingness, in order to be endurable requires those rare ecstatic states with their ascent above space, time, and individuality. These states, in their turn, demand a philosophy which teaches people to use some idea to overcome the unimaginable dreariness of intermediate states. In cases where the political drives are considered unconditionally valid, it's equally necessary for a people to turn to the path of the most extreme forms of secularization. The most magnificent but also the most terrifying example of this is the Roman empire.

Standing between India and Rome and forced to make a tempting choice, the Greeks succeeded in inventing a third form in classical purity. Of course, they did not make use of it for long, but for that very reason they made it immortal. That fact that the darlings of the gods die early holds in all things, but it's equally certain that then they live among the gods for ever. So people should not demand from the noblest thing of all that it should possess the hard-wearing durability of leather—that crude toughness characteristic of the Roman national impulses, for example, probably does not belong to the necessary predicates of perfection.

But if we ask what remedies made it possible for the Greek in their great period, with the extraordinary strength of their Dionysian and political drives, not to exhaust themselves either with an ecstatic brooding or in a consuming pursuit of world power and worldly honour, but to reach that marvelous mixture—just as a noble wine makes one feel fiery and meditative at the same time—then we must keep in mind the immense power of tragedy, which stimulated the entire people, purifying them and giving them release. We will first sense its highest value when it confronts us, as with the Greeks, as the essence of all prophylactic healing potions, as the mediator between the strongest and inherently most disastrous characteristics of a people.

Tragedy draws the highest ecstatic music into itself, so that, with the Greeks, as with us, it immediately brings music to perfection. But then it places the tragic myth and the tragic hero next to the music, who then, like a powerful Titan, takes the whole Dionysian world on his back and thus relieves us of it. On the other hand with the same tragic myth, in the person of the tragic hero, tragedy knows how to redeem us from the avid pressure for this existence and with a warning hand reminds us of another state of being and a higher pleasure for which the struggling hero, full of foreboding, is preparing himself, not through his victory but through his destruction.

Tragedy places between the universal validity of its music and the listener sensitive to the Dionysian an awe-inspiring parable—the myth—and with that gives rise to an illusion, as if the music is only the production's highest device for bringing life to the plastic world of myth. Trusting in this noble deception, tragedy can now move its limbs in the dithyrambic dance and abandon itself unconsciously to an ecstatic feeling of freedom in which it would not dare to revel without that deception.

The myth protects us from the music, while it, by contrast, immediately gives the music its highest freedom. In return, the music gives back to the tragic myth, as a return gift, an urgent and convincing metaphysical significance, of a kind which words and pictures never could attain without its help. And particularly through the music there comes over the spectator of tragedy that certain presentiment of the highest joy, the road to which leads through destruction and negation, so that he thinks what he hears is like the innermost abyss of things speaking to him out loud.

If in these last sentences I have perhaps tried to provide only a provisional expression of this complex idea, something immediately intelligible to few people, at this very point I cannot refrain from encouraging my friends to a further attempt and from asking them to prepare themselves with a single example of our common experience in order to recognize a general principle.

With this example, I must not refer to those who use the images of the action in the scenes—the words and emotions of active people—in order with their help to come closer to the feeling of the music. For none of them speaks music as a mother tongue, and, for all that help, they proceed no further than the lobbies of musical perception, without ever being able to touch its innermost shrine. Some of these who take this road, like Gervinus, don't even succeed in reaching the lobby. But I must turn only to those who have an immediate relationship with music and who find in it, as it were, their mother's womb, those who stand bound up with things almost exclusively through an unconscious musical relationship.

To these true musicians I direct the question: Can they imagine a person capable of perceiving the third act of Tristan and Isolde as an immense symphonic movement, getting no help from words and images, without suffocating from a convulsive spreading of all the wings of his soul? A man who, as in this case, has set his ear, so to speak, on the heart chambers of the world's will, who feels in himself the raging desire for existence pouring forth into all the veins of the world as a thundering rainstorm or as the most delicately spraying brook—would such a man not fall apart on the spot? Could he endure hearing in the suffering glass case of human individuality the echo of countless desires—and cries of woe from the "wide space of the world's night," without, in the midst of this shepherd's medley of metaphysics, inexorably flying off to his original home? But what if nonetheless such a work could be perceived as a totality, without the denial of individual existence, what if such a creation could be produced without shattering its creator—where do we get the solution to such a contradiction?

Here between our highest musical excitement and this music the tragic myth and the tragic hero interpose themselves, basically only as a parable of the most universal facts of all, about which only music can speak directly. However, if we felt as purely Dionysian beings, then myth would be entirely ineffectual as a parable and would remain there beside us unnoticed. It would not make us turn our ears away for an instant from listening to the echo of the universalia ante rem [the universal before the fact].

But here the Apollonian power breaks through, preparing for the reintegration of shattered individuality with the healing balm of blissful illusion. Suddenly we think we see only Tristan, motionless and dazed, as he asks himself, "The old melody—what does it awaken for me?" And what earlier struck us as an empty sigh from the centre of being now only says to us something like "the barren, empty sea." And where we imagined we were dying in a convulsive inner working out of all our feelings with only a little linking us to this existence, now we hear and see only the hero mortally wounded and yet not dying, with his cry full of despair, "Longing! Longing! In death still yearning not to die from yearning!" And when earlier, after such an excess and such a huge number of torments consuming us, the jubilation of the horns, almost like an extreme agony, cuts through our hearts, there stands between us and this "jubilation in itself" the celebrating Kurwenal, turned towards the ship carrying Isolde. No matter how powerful the compassion gripping us inside, in a certain sense, nonetheless, this compassion saves us from the primordial suffering of the world, just as the symbolic picture of myth saves us from the immediate look at the highest world idea, just as thoughts and words save us from the unrestrained outpouring of the unconscious will. Because of that marvelous Apollonian deception it seems to us as if the empire of music confronted us as a plastic world, as if only Tristan's and Isolde's destiny had been formed and stamped out in pictures in the most delicate and expressive of all material.

Thus the Apollonian rescues us from Dionysian universality and delights us with individuals. It attaches our aroused feelings of sympathy to them, and with them it satisfies our sense of beauty, our longing for great and awe-inspiring forms. It presents images of life to us and provokes us to a thoughtful grasp of the kernel of life contained in them. With the immense power of imagery, ideas, ethical instruction, and sympathetic arousal, the Apollonian lifts man up out of his ecstatic self-destruction and blinds him to the universality of the Dionysian process, leading him to the delusion that he is watching just one image of the world (for example, Tristan and Isolde) and that the music only helps him see it better and with greater profundity.

What can the skilful healing power of Apollo's magic not achieve, if it can even excite in us this delusion, so that it seems as if the Dionysian is really working to serve the Apollonian, capable of intensifying its effects—in fact, as if the music was essentially an artistic presentation of an Apollonian content?

With that pre-established harmony which reigns between the perfect drama and its music, drama attains an extreme degree of vividness, something which verbal drama cannot approach. In the independently moving melodic lines all the living forms in the scene simplify themselves into the clarity of curved lines, and the juxtaposition of these lines sounds out to us, sympathizing in the most delicate way with the action as it moves forward. As this happens, the relation of things becomes immediately audible to us in a more sensuously perceptible way, which has nothing abstract about it at all, as we also recognize through it that only in these relations does the essence of a character and of a melodic line clearly reveal itself.

And while the music compels us in this way to see more and more profoundly than ever and the scenic action spreads itself in front of us like a delicate spider's web, our inner view of the world of the stage is infinitely widened and illuminated from within. What could a word poet offer analogous to this—someone who struggles with a very imperfect mechanism in indirect ways to attain with words and ideas that inner expansion of the vivid world of the stage and its inner illumination? Musical tragedy, of course, also uses the word, but at the same time it can set beside it the fundamental basis and origin of that word and reveal to us from inside what that word has become.

But nonetheless we could just as surely claim about this depiction of the action that it is only a marvelous appearance, i.e., that previously mentioned Apollonian delusion, through whose effects we should be relieved of the Dionysian surge and excess. In fact, the relationship between music and drama is fundamentally the reverse—the music is the essential idea of the word, and the drama is only a reflection of this idea, its isolated silhouette.

This identity between the melodic line and the living form, between the harmony and the relations of the characters in that form, is true in an sense opposite to what it might seem to be for us as we look at musical tragedy. We may well stir up the form in the most visible way, enliven and illuminate it from within, but it always remains only an appearance, from which there is no bridge leading to true reality, to the heart of the world. But music speaks out from this heart, and though countless appearances could clothe themselves in the same music, they would never exhaust its essence—they would always be only its external reflection.

And, of course, with the complex relationship between music and drama nothing is explained and everything is confused by the popular and entirely false contrast between the soul and the body. But among our aestheticians it's precisely the unphilosophical crudity of this contrast which seems to have become, for reasons nobody knows, a well known article of faith, while they have learned nothing about the difference between the appearance and the thing-in-itself or, for similarly unknown reasons, don't want to learn anything.

If one result of our analysis might be that the Apollonian in tragedy, thanks to its deception, emerges victorious over the primordial Dionysian elements of music and makes use of these for its own purposes, that is, for the highest dramatic clarity, a very important reservation naturally follows: at the most essential point of all that Apollonian deception is broken up and destroyed. Drama, which, with the help of music, spreads out in front of us with such innerly illuminated clarity in all its movements and forms, as if we were seeing the fabric on the loom while the shuttle moves back and forth, achieves its effect as a totality which lies beyond all the artistic workings of the Apollonian. In the total action of tragedy the Dionysian regains its superiority once more. Tragedy ends with a tone which never could resound from the realm of Apollonian art.

And as that happens, the Apollonian deception reveals itself for what it is, as the veil which, so long as the tragedy is going on, has covered the essentially Dionysian effect. But this Dionysian effect is nonetheless so powerful that at the end it drives the Apollonian drama itself into a sphere where it begins to speak with Dionysian wisdom and where it denies itself and its Apollonian visibility. So we could truly symbolize the complex relationship between the Apollonian and the Dionysian in tragedy with the fraternal bond between both divinities: Dionysus speaks the language of Apollo, but Apollo finally speaks the language of Dionysus, and with that the highest goal of tragedy and art in general is attained.

22

An attentive friend should remind himself, from his own experience, of the pure and unmixed effect of a truly musical tragedy. I think I have described what this effect is like, attending to both aspects of it, so that he will now know how to clarify his own experience for himself. For he will recall how, confronted with the myth unfolding in front of him, he felt himself raised up to some sort of omniscience, as if now the visual power of his eyes was not merely a force dealing with surfaces but was capable of penetrating within, as if, with the help of the music, he could see in front of him the turbulent feelings of the will, the war of motives, the growing storm of passions as something which is, as it were, sensuously present, like an abundance of living lines and figures in motion, and thus as if he could plunge into the most delicate secrets of unknown emotions.

As he becomes conscious of this highest intensification of his instincts which aim for clarity and transfiguration, nonetheless he feels with equal certainty that this long series of Apollonian artistic effects does not produce that delightful indifference of will-less contemplation which the sculptor and the epic poet—that is, the genuine Apollonian artist—bring out in him with their works of art, that is, the justification of the world of the individual attained in that contemplation, which is the peak and essence of Apollonian art. He looks at the transfigured world of the stage and yet denies it.

He sees the tragic hero in front of him in his epic clarity and beauty and, nonetheless, takes pleasure in his destruction. He understands the scenic action to its innermost core, and yet joyfully flies off into the incomprehensible. He feels the actions of the hero as justified and is, nonetheless, still more uplifted when these actions destroy the one who initiated them. He shudders at the suffering which the hero is about to encounter and, nonetheless, because of it has a premonition of a higher, much more overpowering joy. He perceives more things and more profoundly than ever before and yet wishes he were blind.

Where would we be able to derive this miraculous division of the self, this collapse of the Apollonian climax, if not from Dionysian magic, which, while it apparently excites the Apollonian feelings to their highest point, nevertheless can still force this exuberance of Apollonian art into its service? The tragic myth can only be understood as a symbolic picture of Dionysian wisdom by means of Apollonian art. It leads the world of appearances to its limits where it denies itself and once again seeks to fly back into the bosom of the true and single reality, at which point it seems, like Isolde, to sing its metaphysical swan song.

In the surging torrents of seas of my desires, in resounding tones of fragrant waves, in the blowing All of the world's breath— to drown, to sink down to lose consciousness— the highest joy.

So we remember the experiences of the truly aesthetic listener, the tragic artist himself, as he, like a voluptuous divinity of individualism, creates his forms—in which sense his work can scarcely be understood as an "imitation of nature"—and as his immense Dionysian drive then devours this entire world of appearances in order to allow him, through its destruction, to have a premonition of the original and highest artistic joy in the primordial One.

Of course, our aestheticians don't know what to write about this return journey to our original home, about the fraternal bond of the brother gods of art in tragedy, any more than they do about the Apollonian or the Dionysian excitement of the listener, while they never weary of characterizing as the essential feature of the tragic the struggle of the hero with fate, the victory of a moral world order, or the purging of the emotions achieved by tragedy. Such tireless efforts lead me to the thought that in general they may be men incapable of aesthetic excitement, so that when they hear a tragedy perhaps they think of themselves only as moral beings.

Since Aristotle, there has not yet been an explanation of the tragic effect from which one might be able to infer aesthetic conditions or the aesthetic capability of the listener. Sometimes pity and fear are supposed to be pushed by the serious action to an discharge which brings relief. At other times, we are supposed to feel enthusiastic and elevated because of the victory of good and noble principles, by the sacrifice of the hero, taking that as a service to a moral world order.

I have no doubt that for countless men that and only that is precisely the effect of tragedy. But this reveals equally clearly that all these people, together with their aesthetic interpreters, have experienced nothing of tragedy as the highest art. That pathological purgation, the catharsis of Aristotle, which the philologues are uncertain whether to count a medical or a moral phenomenon, brings to mind a remarkable idea of Goethe's. "Without a living pathological interest," he says, "I have also never succeeded in working on any kind of tragic situation, and therefore I prefer to avoid it rather than seek it out. Could it perhaps be the case that among the merits of the ancients the highest degree of the pathetic was also only aesthetic play for them, while with us the truth of nature must be there as well in order for such a work to be produced?"

After our glorious experiences we can now answer yes to this profound question—after we have experienced with wonder precisely this musical tragedy, how truly the highest degree of the pathetic can be, for all that, only an aesthetic game. For that reason, we're justified in claiming that only now can the primordial phenomenon of the tragic be described with some success. Anyone who nowadays still provides explanations in terms of those surrogate effects from spheres beyond aesthetics and doesn't sense that he has risen above the pathological and moralistic processes may well despair of his aesthetic nature. For that condition we recommend as an innocent substitute the interpretation of Shakespeare the way Gervinus does it with the diligent search for "poetic justice."

So with the rebirth of tragedy the aesthetic listener is also born again, in whose place up to this point a strange quid pro quo habitually sat in the theatre space, with half moral and half scholarly demands—the "critic." In his sphere so far everything has been only synthetic and whitewashed with the appearance of life. The performing artist in fact didn't really know what he could begin to do with a listener who behaved so critically, and therefore he, together with dramatist or opera composer who inspired him, peered anxiously for the last remnants of life in this discriminating, barren creature incapable of enjoying itself.

But up to this point the general public has consisted of this sort of "critic." Through education and the press, the student, the school child, indeed even the most harmless female creature has been prepared, without being aware of it, to perceive a work of art in a similar manner. The more noble natures among the artists, faced with such a public, counted on exciting moral and religious forces, and the call for "a moral world view" stepped in vicariously, where, in fact, a powerful artistic magic should have entranced the real listener. Alternatively, dramatists with a pronounced and at least exciting proclivity for contemporary political and social issues brought out such clear productions that the listener could forget his critical exhaustion and let himself go with feelings like patriotism or militaristic moments, or in front of the speaker's desk in parliament or with judicial sentences for crimes and vices. And that necessarily led to an alienation from true artistic purposes and directly to a culture of attitudinizing.

But here there stepped in, what in every artificial art up to now has intervened, a ragingly quick deprivation of that very attitudinizing, so that, for example, the view that the theatre should be used as an institution for the moral education of a people, something taken serious in Schiller's day, is already counted among the incredible antiquities of an education which has been superceded. As the critic came to rule in the theatre and concert and the journalist in the schools and the press in society, art degenerated into an object of entertainment of the basest sort, and the aesthetic critic was used as a way of binding together in a vain, scattered, selfish, and, beyond this, pitifully unoriginal society, of which we can get some sense in Schopenhauer's parable of the porcupines, so there has never been a time when there has been so much chatter about art and when people think so little of it. But can't we still associate with someone who is in a position to entertain himself with Beethoven and Shakespeare? Everyone may answer this question according to his own feelings—with his answer he will at any rate demonstrate what he imagines by the word "culture," provided he seeks to answer the question at all and is not already struck dumb with astonishment.

By contrast, someone with a nobler and more naturally refined ability—even if he also has gradually turned into a critical barbarian in the manner described above—could say something about an unexpected and entirely incomprehsible effect of the sort which something like a happily successful production of Lohengrin had on him, except perhaps he didn't have a hand which could advise him and clearly lead him, so that that incomprehensibly varied and totally incomparable sensation which so shook him at the time remained a single example and, after a short period of illumination, died out, like a mysterious star. That was the moment he had a presentiment of what an aesthetic listener is.

23

Anyone who wants an accurate test for himself to see how closely related he is to the truly aesthetic listener or how much he belongs with the Socratic-critical community could sincerely ask himself about the feelings with which he receives some miracle presented on stage. In that situation, for example, does he feel offended in his historical sense, which organizes itself on strict psychological causality, or does he, in a spirit of generosity, as it were, make a concession to the miracle as something comprehensible in childhood but foreign to him, or does he suffer anything else at all in that process?

For in doing this he will be able to measure how far, in general, he is capable of understanding the myth, the concentrated image of the world, which, as an abbreviation of appearance, cannot work without the miracle. However, it's likely that almost everyone in a strict test would feel himself so thoroughly corrupted by the critical-historical spirit of our culture that he could make the previous existence of the myth credible only with something scholarly, by compromising with some abstractions. However, without myth that culture forfeits its healthy creative natural power: only a horizon reorganized through myth completes the unity of an entire cultural movement.

Through myth all the powers of illusion and of Apollonian dream are first rescued from their random wandering around. The images of myth must be the unseen, omnipresent demonic sentries under whose care the young soul matures and by whose signs a man interprets his life and struggles for himself. Even the state knows no more powerful unwritten laws than the mythical foundation which guarantees its connection to religion, its growth out of mythic ideas.

Alongside that let's now place abstract people, those who are not led by myths, as well as abstract education, abstract customs, abstract law, the abstract state. Let's remember the disorderly roaming of artistic fantasy which is not restrained by any secret myth. Let's imagine a culture which has no fixed and sacred primordial seat but which is condemned to exhaust all possibilities and to live on a meagre diet from all other cultures—and there we have the present, the result of that Socratism whose aim is to destroy myth.

And now the man without a myth stands there, eternally hungry, in the midst of all past ages, rummaging around and digging as he looks for roots, even if he has to shovel for them in the most remote ancient times. What is revealed in the immense historical need of this dissatisfied modern culture, the gathering up of countless other cultures, the consuming desire to know, if not the loss of myth, the loss of the mythic homeland, of the mythic maternal womb?

Let's ask ourselves whether the feverish and eerie inner excitements of this culture is something other than a starving man's greedy snatch and grab for food—and who would still want to give such a culture anything, when nothing which it gobbles down satisfies it and when, at its touch, the most powerful and healthiest nourishment usually changes into "history and criticism."

We would also have to experience painful despair over our German being, if it is already inextricably intermixed in a similar way with its culture, or, indeed, if they have become a single unit, as we can observe, to our horror, with civilized France. What for a long time constituted the great merit of France and the cause of its huge superiority—that very unity of being in people and culture—should make us, when we look at it, praise our luck and give thanks that such a questionable culture has had nothing in common up to this point with the noble core of our people's character.

Instead of that, all our hopes are reaching out yearningly towards the perception that under his restless cultural life jumping around here and there and these cultural convulsions lies hidden a glorious, innerly healthy, and age-old power, which naturally only begins to stir into powerful motion at tremendous moments and then goes on dreaming once again about a future awakening. Out of this abyss the German Reformation arose. In its choral music there rang out for the first time the future style of German music. Luther's choral works sounded as profound, courageous, spiritual, as exhuberantly good and tender as the first Dionysian call rising up out of the thickly growing bushes at the approach of spring. In answer to it came the competing echo of that solemn procession of Dionysian dreamers, whom we have to thank for German music and whom we will thank for the rebirth of the German myth!

I know that now I have to take the sympathetic friend who is following me to a lofty place for lonely contemplation, where he will have only a few travelling companions. By way of encouragement I call out to him that we have to keep hold of those leaders who illuminate the way for us, the Greeks. Up to now in order to purify our aesthetic awareness, we have borrowed from them both of those images of the gods, each of whom rules a specific artistic realm, and by considering Greek tragedy, we came to an awareness of their mutual contact and intensification.

To us the downfall of Greek tragedy must seem to have occurred through a remarkable tearing apart of both of these primordial artistic drives. And this event corresponded to a degeneration and transformation of the character of the Greek people—something which demands from us some serious reflection about how necessarily and closely art and people, myth and custom, tragedy and the state are fundamentally intertwined.

That downfall of tragedy was at the same time the downfall of myth. Up to that point the Greeks were instinctively compelled to tie everything they lived through immediately to their myths—in fact, to understand that experience only through this link. By doing that, even the most recent present moment had to appear to them at once sub species aeterni [under the eye of eternity] and thus, in a certain sense, to be timeless. In this stream of the timeless, however, the state and art both plunged equally, in order to find in it rest from the weight and the greed of the moment. And a people (as well as a person, by the way) is only worth as much as it can stamp upon its experiences the mark of the eternal, for in that way it is, as it were, relieved of the burden of the world and demonstrates its unconscious inner conviction of the relativity of time and of the True, that is, of the metaphysical meaning of life.

Something quite different from this happens when a people begins to understand itself historically and to smash up the mythic bastions standing around it. It is customary for a decisive secularization, a breach with the unconscious metaphysics of its earlier existence, with all the ethical consequences, to be tied in with this process. Greek art and especially Greek tragedy above all checked the destruction of myth. People had to destroy them in order to be able to live detached from their home soil, unrestrained in the wildness of thought, custom, and action.

But now this metaphysical drive still tries to create, even in a toned down form, a transfiguration for itself, in the Socratism of science which pushes toward life. But on the lower steps this very drive led only to a feverish search, which gradually lost itself in a pandemonium of myths and superstitions from all over the place all piled up together. For all that, the Hellene still sat in the middle this pile with an unquenched heart, until he understood to mask that fever, like Graeculus, with Greek cheerfulness and Greek negligence or to plunge completely into some stupefying oriental superstition or other.

In the most obvious way, since the reawakening of Alexandrian-Roman antiquity in the fifteenth century after a long and difficult to describe interval, we have come closer to this condition. Up on the heights this same abundant desire for knowledge, the same dissatisfied happiness in discovery, the same immense secularization, alongside a homeless wandering around, a greedy thronging at foreign tables, a reckless idolizing of the present or a lifeless numbed turning away—with everything sub specie saeculi [under the eye of the secular age], of the "present age."

These same symptoms lead us to suspect the same lack at the heart of this culture—the destruction of myth. It seems hardly possible that transplanting a foreign myth would enjoy any lasting success, without irreparably damaging the tree in the transplant. Perhaps it is at some point strong and healthy enough to slice out this foreign element with a fearful struggle, but usually it must proliferate its diseased condition, sick and faded.

We have such a high regard for the pure and powerful core of the German being that it is precisely there that we dare to expect from it that elimination of powerfully planted foreign elements and consider it possible that the German spirit will come back into an awareness of itself on its own. Perhaps some people will think that this spirit would have start its struggle with the elimination of the Romantic, but at that point he has to remember an external preparation and encouragement in the victorious courage and bloody glory of the recent war and instead search for the inner necessity in the competitive striving always to be worthy of the noble pioneers on this road, including Luther just as much as our great artists and poets.

But let him never believe that he can fight such a battle without his house gods, without his mythic homeland, without a "bringing back" of all German things! And if the German in his hesitation should look around him for a leader who will take him back again to his long lost home land, whose roads and pathways he hardly knows any more, let him only listen to the sweet enticing call of the Dionysian bird hovering above him seeking to show him the way.

24

Among the characteristic artistic effects of musical tragedy we had to stress an Apollonian illusion through which we are supposedly rescued from immediate unity of being with the Dionysian music, while our musical excitement can discharge itself in an Apollonian sphere, in a visible middle world which interposed itself. By doing this we thought we had noticed how, through this discharge, that this middle world of the scenic action, the drama in general, to a certain degree became visible and comprehensible from within, in a way which is unattainable in all other Apollonian art. Hence, it was here, where the Apollonian is energized and raised aloft, as it were, through the spirit of the music, we had to recognize the highest intensification of its power and, therefore, in the fraternal bond of Apollo and Dionysus, the highest point of both Apollonian and Dionysian artistic aims.

Of course, the projected Apollonian image with this inner illumination through music does not achieve the effect characteristic of the weaker degrees of Apollonian art—what epic or animated stone are capable of, compelling the contemplating eye to that calm delight in the world of the individual. In spite of a higher animation and clarity, that effect will not permit itself to be attained.

We looked at drama and with a penetrating gaze, forced our way into the inner moving world of its motives—and nonetheless for us it was as if only an allegorical picture passed before us, whose most profound meaning we thought we could almost guess and which we wanted to pull aside, like a curtain, in order to look at the primordial image behind it. The brightest clarity of the image did not satisfy us. For this seemed to hide just as much as it revealed. And while, with its allegorical-like revelation, it seemed to promise to rip aside the veil, to disclose the mysterious background, once again that penetrating light illuminating everything held the eye in its spell and held it from penetrating any more deeply.

Anyone who has not had the experience of having to watch and, at the same time, of yearning to go above and beyond watching will have difficulty imagining how definitely and clearly these two processes exist together and are felt alongside each other as one observes the tragic myth. However, the truly aesthetic spectators will confirm for me that among the peculiar effects of tragedy this co-existence may be the most remarkable.

If we now translate this phenomenon going on in the aesthetic spectator into an analogous process in the tragic artist, we will have understood the genesis of the tragic myth. He shares with the Apollonian sphere of art the full joy in appearances and in watching—at the same time he denies this joy and has an even higher satisfaction in the destruction of the visible world of appearances.

The content of the tragic myth is at first an epic event with the glorification of the struggling hero. But what is the origin of that inherently mysterious feature, the fact that the suffering in the fate of the hero, the most painful victories, the most agonizing opposition of motives, in short, the exemplification of that wisdom of Silenus, or, expressing it aesthetically, of the ugly and dissonant, in so many countless forms, is presented with such fondness, always renewed—and precisely in the richest and youngest age of a people? Do we not perceive in all this a higher pleasure?

For the fact that in life things are really so tragic would at least account for the development of an art form—if art is not only an imitation of natural reality but a metaphysical supplement to that reality, set beside it in order to overcome it. And the tragic myth, in so far as it belongs to art at all, also participates fully in this general purpose of art to provide metaphysical transfiguration. But what does it transfigure, when it leads out the world of appearance in the image of the suffering hero? Least of all the "Reality" of this world of appearances, for it says directly to us: "Look here! Look right here! This is your life! Tis is the hour hand on the clock of your existence!"

And does the myth show us this life in order to transfigure it for us? If not, in what does the aesthetic joy consist with which we also allow these images to pass in front of us? I ask about aesthetic delight and know full well that many of these images can in addition now and then still produce a moral pleasure, for example, in the form of pity or a moral triumph. But whoever wants to derive the effect of the tragic merely from these moral origins—as, of course, has been customary in aesthetics for far too long—should not think that he has then done anything for art, which above all must demand purity in its realm. For an explanation of the tragic myth the very first demand is that he seek that joy characteristic of it in the purely aesthetic sphere, without reaching over into the territory of pity, fear, and the morally sublime. How can the ugly and dissonant, the content of the tragic myth, excite an aesthetic delight?

Here it is necessary for us to vault with a bold leap into a metaphysics of art, in which I repeat an earlier sentence—that existence and the world appear justified only as an aesthetic phenomenon. It's in this sense that the tragic myth has to convince us that even the ugly and dissonant are an artistic game, which the will, in the eternal abundance of its joy, plays with itself. But there's a direct way to make this primordial phenomenon of Dionysian art, so difficult to comprehend, completely understandable and to enable one to grasp it immediately—through the miraculous meaning of musical dissonance, the way the music, set next to the world, is the only thing that can give an idea of what it means to understand a justification of the world as an aesthetic phenomenon. The joy which the tragic myth produces has the same homeland as the delightful sensation of dissonance in music. The Dionysian, together with its primordial joy felt even in pain, is the common birth womb of music and the tragic myth.

Thus, shouldn't we have made that difficult problem of the tragic effect really much easier now that we have called on the relation of musical dissonance to help us? For now we understand what it means in tragedy to want to keep looking and at the same time to yearn for something beyond what we see. We would have to characterize this condition in relation to the artistic use of dissonance precisely as the fact that we want to keep listening and at the same time yearn to get beyond what we hear.

That striving for the infinite, the wing beat of longing, associated with the highest delight in clearly perceived reality, reminds us that in both states we must recognize a Dionysian phenomenon, which always reveals to us all over again the playful cracking apart and destruction of the world of the individual as the discharge of primordial delight, in a manner similar to the one in which gloomy Heraclitus compares the force constructing the world to a child who playfully sets stones here and there, builds sand piles, and then knocks them down again.

And thus in order to assess the Dionysian capability of a people correctly, we have to think not just about their music; we must also to think about their tragic myth as the second feature of that capacity. Given this closest of relationships between music and myth, now we can in a similar way assume that a degeneration or deprivation of one of them will be linked to a decline in the other, if a weakening of myth in general manifests itself in a weakening of the Dionysian capability.

But concerning both of these, a look at the development of the German being should leave us in no doubt: in the opera as well as in the abstract character of our myth-deprived existence, in an art which has sunk down to mere entertainment as well as in a life guided by concepts, that inartistic and equally life-draining nature of Socratic optimism stands revealed.

For our consolation, however, there are indications that in spite of everything the German spirit rests and dreams in magnificent health, its profundity and Dionysian power undamaged, like a knight sunk down in slumber in an inaccessible abyss. And from this abyss, the Dionysian song rises up to us in order to make us understand that this German knight is also still dreaming his age-old Dionysian myth in solemn blissful visions. Let no one believe that the German spirit has lost for ever its mythic homeland, when it still understands so clearly the voice of the birds which tell of that homeland. One day it will find itself awake in all the morning freshness of an immense sleep. Then it will kill dragons, destroy the crafty dwarf, and awake Brunnhilde—and even Wotan's spear itself will not be able to block its way.

My friends, you who have faith in Dionysian music, you also know what tragedy means to us. In it we have the tragic myth, reborn from music—and in it you must hope for everything and forget what is most distressing! The most painful thing, however, for all of us is this—the long degradation under which the German genius, alienated from house and home, has lived in service to that crafty dwarf. You understand my words—as you also will understand my hopes as I conclude.

25

Music and tragic myth are equally an expression of the Dionysian capacity of a people and are inseparable from each other. Both derive from an artistic realm that lies beyond the Apollonian. Both transfigure a region in whose joyful chords dissonance as well as the terrible image of world fade delightfully away. Both play with the sting of joylessness, trusting in the extreme power of their magical arts. Through this play both justify the existence of even the "worst of worlds." Here the Dionysian shows itself, measured against the Apollonian, as the eternal and primordial artistic force, which summons the entire world of appearances into existence. In its midst a new transfiguring illusion becomes necessary in order to keep alive the living world of the individual. Could we imagine some human development of dissonance—and what is a man other than that?—then this dissonance, in order to capable of life, would need a marvelous illusion, which covered it with a veil of beauty over its essential being. This is the true artistic purpose of Apollo, in whose name we put together all those countless illusions of beautiful appearances which render existence at every moment in general worth living and push us to experience the next moment.

But in this process, from that basis for all existence, the Dionysian bed rock of the world, only as much can come into the consciousness of the human individual as can be overcome once more by that Apollonian power of transfiguration, so that both of these artistic drives are compelled to display their powers in a strictly mutual proportion, in accordance with the law of eternal justice. Where Dionysian power rises up as impetuously as we are seeing it rise, there Apollo must already have come down to us, hidden in a cloud. The next generation may well see the richest his beautiful effects.

However, the fact that this effect is necessary each man will experience most surely through his intuition, if he once, even in a dream, feels himself set back into the life of the ancient Greeks. As he wanders under high Ionic colonnades, glancing upwards to a horizon marked off with pure and noble lines, with reflections of his transfigured form beside him in shining marble, around him people solemnly striding or moving delicately, with harmoniously sounding lutes and a speech of rhythmic gestures—faced with this constant stream of beauty, would he not have to extend his hand to Apollo and cry out: "Blessed Hellenic people! How great Dionysus must be among you, if the Delphic god thinks such magic necessary to heal your dithyrambic madness!" To a person in such a mood as this, however, an old Athenian, looking at him with the noble eye of Aeschylus, might reply: "But, you strange foreigner, how much must these people have suffered in order to be able to become so beautiful! But now follow me to the tragedy and sacrifice with me in the temple of both divinities."

www.ingramcontent.com/pod-product-compliance
Lightning Source LLC
Chambersburg PA
CBHW031651040426
42453CB00006B/265